For Zion's Sake

For Zion's Sake

Lance Lambert

LANCE LAMBERT MINISTRIES

Richmond, Virginia, USA

ISBN: 978-1-68389-201-4

www.lancelambert.org

Contents

Introduction

For Zion's Sake originated with a series of messages Lance gave at Halford House in Richmond, Surrey, England. We believe these messages were given before his move to Jerusalem in 1980, yet we are unaware of the more precise dates.

As you will see from reading these chapters, *Zion* is much more than a mountain, a concept, or only something relative to the Jewish people. Zion is quite a main topic in the living Word of God. This topic is worthy of our consideration as we wait for His soon return. Be encouraged as you read, and hear what the Lord has to say about *His Zion*.

1.
The Battle

Isaiah 58

Cry aloud, spare not, lift up thy voice like a trumpet, and declare unto my people their transgression, and to the house of Jacob their sins. Yet they seek me daily, and delight to know my ways: as a nation that did righteousness, and forsook not the ordinance of their God, they ask of me righteous judgments; they delight to draw near unto God. Wherefore have we fasted, say they, and thou seest not? wherefore have we afflicted our soul, and thou takest no knowledge? Behold, in the day of your fast ye find your own pleasure, and exact all your labours. Behold, ye fast for strife and contention, and to smite with the fist of wickedness: ye fast not this day so as to make your voice to be heard on high. Is such the fast that I have chosen? the day for a man to afflict his soul? Is it to bow down his head as a rush, and to spread sackcloth and ashes under him? wilt thou call this a fast, and an acceptable day to the Lord? Is not this the fast that I have chosen: to loose the bonds of wickedness, to undo the bands of the yoke, and to let the oppressed go free, and that ye break every yoke? Is it not to deal thy bread to the hungry, and that thou bring the poor that are cast out to thy house? when thou seest the naked, that thou cover him; and that thou hide not thyself from thine own flesh? Then shall thy light break forth as the morning, and thy healing shall spring forth speedily; and thy righteousness shall go before thee; the glory of the Lord shall be thy rearward. Then shalt thou call, and the Lord will answer; thou shalt cry, and he will say, Here I am.

If thou take away from the midst of thee the yoke, the putting forth of the finger, and speaking wickedly; and if thou draw out thy soul to the hungry, and satisfy the afflicted soul: then shall thy light rise in darkness, and thine obscurity be as the noonday; and the Lord will guide thee continually, and satisfy thy soul in dry places, and make strong thy bones; and thou shalt be like a watered garden, and like a spring of water, whose waters fail not. And they that shall be of thee shall build the old waste places; thou shalt raise up the foundations of many generations; and thou shalt be called The repairer of the breach, The restorer of paths to dwell in.

If thou turn away thy foot from the sabbath, from doing thy pleasure on my holy day; and call the sabbath a delight, and the holy of the Lord honourable; and shalt honour it, not doing thine own ways, nor finding thine own pleasure, nor speaking thine own words: then shalt thou delight thyself in the Lord; and I will make thee to ride upon the high places of the earth; and I

There is a very well-known phrase in Isaiah 62:1 that I would like to take as the theme verse for our times together: "For Zion's sake will I not hold my peace, and for Jerusalem's sake I will not rest until her righteousness goes forth as brightness and her salvation as a lamp that burneth."

These are wonderful words. They are the words of the Messiah Himself; they are not the words of the prophet Isaiah. If you look back in chapter 61:1 you see "the Spirit of the Lord God is upon Me," and you know that is the Messiah speaking. Then when you come to chapter 62, you have the Lord Jesus Himself speaking, "For Zion's sake will I not hold My peace and for Jerusalem's sake I will not rest until her righteousness goes forth as brightness and her salvation as a lamp that burneth." So, I believe that in some way the Lord would direct our attention to what this Zion really is, into which the Lord has called us, and over which our Lord has such a travail in His Spirit, for which He intercedes even now at the right hand of God the Father. May God give us that spirit of wisdom and revelation in this matter for we are touching the heart of the whole purpose of God when we touch this.

I included that 58th chapter of Isaiah because that chapter has been very, very much on my heart in a very living way. We will not come to it now, but I have read it because it underlies all that we shall say. In the end we will come to it and we shall look at it very closely. I believe, that if the Lord will help us, we shall see what it has to do with the building up of Zion, the building up of that Jerusalem of God.

Now I would like to turn you to another part of the Word in the Psalms, Psalm 2.

Why do the nations rage,
And the peoples meditate a vain thing?
The kings of the earth set themselves,
And the rulers take counsel together,
Against the Lord, and against his anointed, [That word is His Messiah, His Anointed; in Hebrew His *Messiah* or His Christ]
saying,
Let us break their bonds asunder,
And cast away their cords from us.
He that sitteth in the heavens will laugh:
The Lord will have them in derision.
Then will he speak unto them in his wrath,
And vex them in his sore displeasure:
Yet I have set my king upon my holy hill of Zion.
I will tell of the decree: the Lord said unto me, Thou art my son;
This day have I begotten thee.
Ask of me, and I will give thee the nations for thine inheritance,
And the uttermost parts of the earth for thy possession.
Thou shalt break them with a rod of iron;
Thou shalt dash them in pieces like a potter's vessel.
Now therefore be wise, O ye kings:
Be instructed, ye judges of the earth.
Serve the Lord with fear,
And rejoice with trembling.

Kiss the son, lest he be angry, and ye perish in the way,
For his wrath will soon be kindled.
Blessed are all they that take refuge in him.

This second Psalm, so well-known, is what we call a Messianic Psalm. That is, it is a Psalm that is prophetic. It is a prediction of the coming of the Messiah Jesus. It is quoted a number of times in the New Testament. It is quoted, for instance, in the letter of the Hebrews at least twice. It is quoted by Paul in that tremendous address he gave in Acts 13. It is quoted in some other places in the New Testament.

It contains vitally important truth relating to the purpose of God in this age and the conflict over it. It is as if the Lord draws aside the veil for a little while to allow His redeemed ones to understand what it is that they have been brought into, why things go wrong, why the inexplicable comes into our lives, why it is we have to battle through in prayer. Why do we speak so much about warfare, about having to intercede, about having to get behind the scenes? Perhaps you younger ones, and some of you older ones as well, have wondered, "Well, what is it all really about? Are we in a fool's paradise? Are we sort of deceived? Are we being led along by some strange, hallucinatory power? What is it all for?"

In this Psalm, the veil is drawn aside and it is like a little glimpse into what lies behind the scenes. It is as if the Lord shows us for a second what our salvation has introduced us into, what it has brought us into. It is tremendous really! This little Psalm, so well-known, contains vitally important truth because it covers the whole of the age, not only this age but in fact other ages of time, too. It gives us an idea, as it were, of what the Lord has sought to do and is doing and why there is this great battle over it.

Now having said that, I would like to underline it even further. It has particular relevance for the end of the age because if this battle over God's anointed, over His purpose—the declared will of God and its fulfilment—is so tremendous, it stands to reason that the nearer we get to the end of the age, the greater will be that conflict and battle. It will, as it were, build up to its climax.

I believe, therefore, that this little Psalm has particular relevance for us as we live, we believe, at the end of the age. We do not know how far off the Lord's coming is. We have our suspicions, but the fact is we are far nearer to His coming than those who first believed, and we must be very far on into the age, surely. If we take some of the signs which are being fulfilled then we have milestones, as it were, which no other generation of believers has had before. Milestones which are quite clearly fulfilled prophecy and are an indication of where we are, approximately, in this age. If that is so, I think that this Psalm is a tremendous introduction to looking at this whole matter of the Lord's concern for Zion and for Jerusalem.

Why Do the Nations Rage?

First of all, let me underline the battle which rages over the purpose of God. Look at this Psalm: nations, peoples, kings, and rulers. Notice what it says: They rage against the Lord and against His anointed. Here we have the first great thing about this battle: it is not firstly to do with you and me! We are small fry! We are no problem to the enemy. If the Lord were to leave us, there is not a single person in this room who would not become a captive of the enemy within a matter of days. We are nothing in ourselves and the fact that we are in a conflict and in a battle is not because, we, you or I, are significant people, that somehow or other we are very important people, or that we are at great turning points in the purpose of God. Put all that out of your head. As I have often said, I have met so many of the 'two witnesses' that are mentioned in the book of Revelation chapter 11, I could honestly fill Saint Paul's Cathedral with them! I could have a congregation of those people who believe they are the witnesses from Revelation 11. Just recently there is a man who has been sitting in the garden tomb for the last few months who believes he is one of the witnesses from Revelation. He is quite a nice gentleman. His wife is the other witness. It is quite amazing how people believe that they are the witness. Now, we want to put all that out of our heads.

This battle is supremely directed against the Lord and against His Messiah. Insofar as you and I have been delivered from the power of darkness and transferred into the kingdom of God's dear Son, we become significant as far as the enemy is concerned. Because we are trophies of God's grace, we have been transferred out of one domain into another, out of one man into another, out of one creation into another, and out of one whole order and system into another.

Now, that is what baptism really is all about. When a person is baptised, it is not just simply saying, "I want to follow the Lord." What they are really saying is, "As Jesus was crucified and buried and raised again on the third day, so through His crucifixion, I have been crucified. I have died with Him and when He was buried, I was buried with Him. When He was raised from the dead, I was raised to walk in newness of life. I have been transferred out of one whole domain into another. Out of one authority into another authority."

Now, insofar as you are a child of God, insofar as you have been born of the Spirit, insofar as you have come into—by the grace of God—a covenant relationship with the Lord, then you are significant in the eyes of the enemy. Should there be anyone here tempted to go back into the world, do not think, "Well, you know, it would be a much easier thing if I were just to go back into the world. Things are much easier there. Why persevere, why endure, why go through all this sort of routine, year in, year out? I see other friends who seem to be having such a happy and giddy time. I think it would be easier."

It will be easier, I promise you. It will be easier for precisely the first year or two required to blind you and deceive you. But once you have been alienated from the Lord and from His people, then the enemy will come in. He will pursue you and pursue you and pursue you because you can never switch your sides. Once the Lord has made you His, you are stamped with the mark of the Lord and the devil knows it. That is why you will never find a backslider whose way has been happy. In the end it is a terrible way, a way of destruction, a way of devouring, a way of unhappiness, a way of tragedy—always—of aimlessness, of a life wasted. It is as if the enemy will do every single thing in his power just to cruelly afflict that life because that one has belonged to the Lord. How stupid we are when we listen to those whisperings of the enemy that if we were to forsake the Lord and go back it would be easier.

I remember years ago, a couple of brothers who fell out with everybody—we were quite small in those days—and then they got a revelation that we were all of the devil. It was quite a revelation. I remember they went to a friend of ours (not too good a friend) and they poured out to him how they got this revelation. He tended to support them, part-way anyway, and then they said, "This is the evidence: ever since we have seen that it is of the devil, we have been able to get up at 5 o'clock in the morning and have two hours of quiet time and it has been bliss!"

Now this "friend" was deeply impressed and trotted round to me to tell me how he felt that really here was evidence for something. I mean, there was something really wrong with us. "This is the thing; we all have such a battle to get up, don't we?" he said, looking at me very piercingly. He said, "These get up at five for two hours of prayer and it is absolute bliss."

We could not say a thing. At the time I really wondered whether we were deceived. I thought, "Well, we have such a battle to really pray for half an hour, let alone two hours. These had the same battle a month ago when they were with us, but now there is no battle. It's all glory. It's all bliss."

Six months later they had both backslidden. So much for the two hours. Of course, I woke up then and I thought: "Of course, if I had been the enemy that is what I would have done. As soon as you can get a person out, remove all the antagonism, remove all the blockage, remove all the frustrating tactics and remove all the sort of wearing out processes and thus give them a good time. Just let them flow along! Because we've got 'em!"

You see dear friends, the first thing we want to see about this battle, which is raging over the purpose of the Lord, is that it is against the Lord and against His Messiah—His Christ. Then, insofar as you and I have been joined to the Messiah and become part of the Messiah, we are in the battle. Now, I find this is a great comfort because if I thought the battle was supremely to do with me, I really would be very worried. Wouldn't you? Well, I would. I would be quite bothered if I thought that I was really the target of the whole thing. I would think: "Oh what a responsibility I have got." But when I know that the *real target* is the Lord and His anointed, it gives me great comfort. You have to be very, very self-centred and proud and bigoted to believe, as the enemy does, as the devil does, that he can outwit God. We know who is on the winning side. We know who has the victory in this. So there we are.

The Nations Rage and the Peoples Meditate a Vain Thing

Now, would you also look at the words that are used here? They are very expressive words. "Why do the nations rage and the peoples meditate a vain thing? The kings of the earth set themselves and the rulers take counsel together." This word is translated as *rage* here, this Hebrew word, is *to be in tumult or commotion*. Why are the nations in *tumult*? Why are they in *commotion*? The word *rage* is a very good word. It means: why are the nations seething? Why are they all in a great, restless, seething mass backwards and forwards?

Then, "Why do the peoples meditate a vain thing?" Again, this word *meditate* is actually *to imagine* as in the old Authorised Version. Or *devise*—why do the people's *devise* a vain thing? The word is: an *empty thing*, a *vanity*, an *emptiness*.

Here is something very interesting. You have, in these few verses, the whole collision between the kingdom of this world and the kingdom of God, between the powers of darkness and the kingdom of heaven. You have just in these verses the whole collision! Because you see it is Babylon versus Jerusalem. One thing is, not just the imagination, but the devising, the scheming of a whole system, of a whole philosophy, of a whole way of life, of a whole city, of a whole society that can exist without God. It can take the name of God, but it is not founded in God. Its origin is not in God. Do you understand? You have got it all here in this word, *imagine a vain thing*. It does not just mean that they are empty-headed. It means that these peoples of these nations in their seething discontent and rebellion against the Lord and against His purpose have got another idea. It is not that they are just *against* the Lord, they have something they want to substitute *for* the Lord. They want an altogether different way of life, a different system of doing things.

In a few moments we shall come right up to the present time, because that is exactly what is emerging in our society, as it has been called, officially, the *Post-Christian Era*. Now it is all coming out into the open—another type of unit of society. We do not want marriage. We do not need chastity. We do not need men and women. (As you know, in Sweden they have just introduced a law, or are seeking to introduce a law to allow there to be homosexual marriages and allow either homosexual women or homosexual men to adopt children and bring them up.) It is incredible! This will be followed by one thing after another. This is the alternative society. This is the new society, the new morality. We can do away with the Judao-Christian concept of the family, of marriage, of chastity before marriage, of two people, meant for each other to remain with each other for life. We can do away with it. So you see, dear friends, this is not quite so old fashioned, or all up in the air as it may seem at first. It is not so at all.

The Kings Set Themselves

Now you notice also this word *to set themselves*. It says: "The kings of the earth set themselves and the rulers take counsel together." This word *set themselves* is exactly really as it is translated, *to station oneself* or *to take one's stand*. It is something to do with battle. You take your stance, or you take your position, or you take your stand in battle. So, you see, this is not just an empty-headed rebellion. These nations, these peoples are inspired by an infernal mind, by an infernal intelligence, by a hellish intelligence and the whole idea and aim is somehow or other to take their stand against God, to take their position against God with an alternative to the whole.

The Rulers Take Counsel Together

Then you continue and you find this *taking counsel together* is a very interesting little word. It is *to establish* or *to found* or *to fix*. It means in this connection, to seat themselves close together, to sit in conclave. So, you see you have got a marvellous picture of something in the whole world. It is not flesh and blood. There is something behind it.

Let Us Break Their Bonds Asunder

Now, you continue and you will notice that it is rebellion against the Lord and against His Messiah which is at the heart of the whole matter. "Let us break their bonds asunder and cast away their cords from us" (v. 3). Now that is the heart of the matter. It has been, as it were, in our society right from the beginning. Whether we call it so-called Christian society, or pre-Christian society, or the post-Christian society, the fact of the matter is that this spirit of lawlessness has been there, though restrained, all the way through.

Of course, it speaks of it in II Thessalonians 2:7–12:

For the mystery of lawlessness doth already work: only there is one that restraineth now, until he be taken out of the way. And then shall be revealed the lawless one, whom the Lord Jesus shall slay with the breath of his mouth, and bring to nought by the manifestation of his coming; even he, whose coming is according to the working of Satan with all power and signs and lying wonders, and with all deceit of unrighteousness for them that perish; because they received not the love of the truth, that they might be saved. And for this cause God sendeth them a working of error, that they should believe a lie: that they all might be judged who believed not the truth, but had pleasure in unrighteousness.

Now, we have two things there. We have "the mystery of lawlessness," this mystery being something invisible, something not manifest, the mystery of lawlessness, which explains the whole of human history. It explains why, with all the multitudes of human beings who have longed for peace, for unity, for justice, for equality, for some kind of life that is worth living; in spite of it all, all through the thousands of years, we have had nothing but war, nothing but injustice, nothing but inequality, nothing but unhappiness. It is the mystery of lawlessness which has poisoned the whole of human society and the whole of this system that has grown out of it.

However, now at the end of the age, "the lawless one" will appear. So, it is not only a spirit of lawlessness, but in the end there is going to appear the lawless one who is the antichrist. We are told that with the antichrist there will come all kinds of strange things. There will be signs and wonders—lying wonders and signs—and a delusion and many other things.

Now, the reason that I am stressing this is this: behind flesh and blood, behind ideologies and philosophies, behind theories such as Darwinism and many other theories which now, literally, are the basis for most of the behaviour of our society, there are principalities and powers and world rulers of darkness.

Some of you may be a bit surprised by what I have said about Darwinism. I don't know too much. I am not a scientist and I have never had to study in-depth Darwinian theory. But this I do know: the liquidation under Adolf Hitler of the mentally retarded, leading later to genocide—the destruction of the Jewish people and also, in the end, was going to be the destruction of the Slav people as sub-human—was all based on Darwinian, evolutionary theory. In other words, man has not got a spirit; he is just an animal. Just like you exterminate vermin, just like you exterminate flies, so you can exterminate a whole class of persons.

Now, you know, this is exactly why we are coming up against it again—mercy killing, euthanasia, abortion, all kinds of things. What lies behind it? Well, if we are only the human animal, if that is all we really are, a super-animal, of course you can do these things. It is the best thing to do, isn't it? Just wipe out this and wipe out that. We do that with pedigree stocks of cattle, or sheep or dogs or cats and so on, so why not with human beings?

That is what I mean when I say that behind flesh and blood, behind these ideologies, behind these philosophies, behind many of these seemingly so clever, so reasoned theories, lie principalities and powers. There may be in some of them more than a spark of truth, but the work of the enemy is to, as it were, use it in such a way that it leads to destruction and corruption and death. It is not only behind such things like that but behind political movements and systems you also have these beings.

Of course, the apostle Paul speaks about this in well-known words in Ephesians 6:12, "For our wrestling is not against flesh and blood, but against principalities, against the powers, against the world-rulers of this darkness, against hosts of wicked spirits in the heavenly places." We know also of II Corinthians 10:4–5, "For the weapons of our warfare are not of the flesh, but mighty through God to the casting down of strongholds, casting down imaginations" (*Imaginations* is the old word, *speculations* is perhaps an even better word), "and every high thing that is exalted against the knowledge of God, and bringing into captivity every thought to the obedience of Christ."

Either we really believe these things, or we don't. Are these things just a bit of theory which we all believe because we feel it is incumbent upon us as Christians, as born again believers to believe the Bible? So we say, "Well, we've got to believe that because it's true." Either we believe it in that kind of haphazard way, or we really do believe that this book is the revelation of truth. If it really is the revelation of truth, then we are not wrestling against flesh and blood but against principalities.

"Principalities" are princes. "Powers, authorities," are those which have authority over things. "Against world-rulers of this darkness," does not mean the physical darkness but spiritual, moral darkness. "Against hosts of wicked spirits in the heavenlies." When we go over to II Corinthians 10, we are not dealing with the people. We are dealing with what these beings have produced– namely, strongholds or fortresses. These beings have got strong points. They have strongholds in certain areas, in certain nations, in certain societies, in certain political movements, and in certain ideologies. They have formed and produced and created strongholds. They have produced speculative theories or philosophies which have captured thousands and thousands of minds.

Think of Chairman Mao's thoughts. Thousands of minds just captured by speculative philosophy, by high things exalted against the knowledge of God. Forgive me for coming back to it and giving it a hammering here, but like the Darwinian theory, it is something so clever, so highly intelligent but apparently against the knowledge of God, so much so that many find it hard to really go through with the Lord. Shall we put it this way? They find it hard to trust in the complete authority and inspiration of the Word of God because of this theory. Now, I have no doubt that others could help you a good deal more than I can on the whole matter of this theory. As we have often discussed it in times past, I believe that in Genesis 1 there is some form of evolution, certainly within the Hebrew, but not as far as man is concerned. It is only within the species. However, that would be another study altogether.

My point is that this is something so engineered and produced by the enemy that it is an onslaught and assault upon the knowledge of God. Thoughts. Where do these thoughts come from? Where did the thought come from in Marx's mind that was to capture half of the world? Where did the thought come from in Mohammad's mind that was to capture half of the world? Where did these thoughts come from?

In other words, there is something behind these nations' seething commotion, behind these peoples scheming and devising an emptiness, as far as God is concerned, something that has highfalutin phrases and ideas within it, but which, in the end, ends up in a dungeon of misery. This setting of the kings, their stationing of themselves and the rulers going into conclave together against the Lord and against His anointed saying, "Let us break their bonds asunder" (Psalm 2:3), anyone who knows the Lord knows there are no bonds with the Lord. You have never had your self-centredness dealt with if you feel you are in bondage as far as the Lord is concerned. Or "cast away their cords." The only cords I have ever known the Lord put 'round me were the cords of love by which He has drawn me to Himself. I know no others.

Now I am not saying that we believers do not make truth into a dreadful bondage. My goodness! I go around to some of them and I have not seen a more drab lot in all my life. They look so sunken in the cheek and pale in the skin and dark in attire. Oh dear, the dear Lord's people ... How we get into bondage as soon as we get some truth instead of letting it come to us livingly in the power of the Spirit as something that is liberating. We turn it into a system and then we make it a bondage. However, there is no bondage with the Lord, only the bondage of His love. Of course, if you have your own ideas and they clash with Him, then there is going to be some talk of bondage somewhere. If you feel that you begin to understand His will for your life and your future, and you do not like it, I can understand you thinking about "casting away the cords." But if you have settled it in your heart and your life that you are going to be His, and that His way is best, and that He loves you so much that He will only ever lead you into what is the highest and best and fullest for you, then my dear friend there is no bondage and there are no cords.

You see, this matter is far more important than perhaps you and I realise. We must expect far greater conflict and more evidence of this rebellion as we move toward the end of the age. In the book of Revelation, it says that at the end there will come out, as it were, these unclean frogs, described as full of demons that will go out to deceive the whole earth. Well, that doesn't sound very pleasant, does it? I mean, I am quite fond of frogs. We have tried to do our part in preserving them in this garden and we have quite a lot of them hopping all over the place much to the upset of some, but it is not a very nice description which we read in Revelation 16:13–16.

And I saw coming out of the mouth of the dragon, and out of the mouth of the beast, and out of the mouth of the false prophet, three unclean spirits, as it were frogs: for they are spirits of demons, working signs; which go forth unto the kings of the whole world, to gather them together unto the war of the great day of God, the Almighty. (Behold, I come as a thief. Blessed is he that watcheth, and keepeth his garments, lest he walk naked, and they see his shame.) And they gathered them together into the place which is called in Hebrew Har-Magedon.

Well, I must say that doesn't sound a very pleasant description of what is going to happen at the end. In other words, it is a very imaginative, a very evocative description of a reality, of systems of ideologies that are founded in spiritual beings that are going to come out at the end.

Now, if we are honest with ourselves, don't you really feel that we are fast moving into this era now? I have never before known the Lord's people so tired. I do not mean here; I mean everywhere. When we were together just recently, the intercessors, leaders from all over the world, from New Zealand, Australia, Canada, the United States, South Africa, Scandinavia and so on, it was amazing to hear the reports being given. It is as if the people of God all over the world are facing quite a new dimension of spiritual activity. Well, are we going to be afraid? I mean, I do not see why we should be afraid. People become so afraid about all these things. They say, "I don't like him speaking about things like that. Why can't we have something helpful? I mean, to talk about dragons and demons and ideologies and all those unclean things going all over the earth—it doesn't help."

A lady said to me a while ago, "I couldn't bear it, talking about the possibility of a third world war." She said, "I think we have all got to be raptured before then!"

Well, I said to her, "I hope you are." But I said, "We have no guarantee from the Word of God that we are going to be raptured before a third world war. I can't find it."

You may know dear Phyllis Thompson, who has written a number of books. She was out in Jerusalem recently and a bomb had just gone off in one of the souks. A friend was saying to her, "Now, Phyllis, keep your eyes open. If you see any bag around, just move out of the way swiftly if it is lying next to a door or next to a window."

So Phyllis asked, "Why?"

"Well," he said, "It's a bomb in it!" Then he said, "You don't want to be blown up, do you?"

Good for ol' Phyllis, do you know what she said? She said, "I'd much rather be blown into the kingdom than eke it out in an old age home!"

I said to her, "Good for you, Phyllis! That's the spirit!"

What is the real difference? Sometimes I think it might be a lot easier to be blown into the kingdom, don't you? Just get *blooowwn* into the kingdom just like that! Instead of having to have years and years and years of just fading out! I mean, there is something to be said for it. When people say to me they are frightened to death of nuclear bombs and all of it, what is there to be afraid of? If you are joined to the eternal Messiah, how on earth can a nuclear bomb do anything to you? What is the real difference if you died 2000 years ago and your body has long since gone to dust? What is the real difference in having your body blown up? When the Lord brings about a resurrection body it will be just the same miracle. He can bring the molecules together again. Now, I don't know why everyone gets frightened over this. It is not a very nice prospect, but it will be over so quickly. Of course, we hope that the Lord will take us before this, but if we have to go that way, we are going to go that way. Why should we be afraid of it? We have a Lord who is bigger than any bombs.

It is a wonderful thing then to remember that however we are moving into this last phase of the age, we can thank God, in this great conflict and battle that is raging over the purpose of God, it is against the Lord and against His anointed. Therefore, we know who is going to win! If it was against us, you and me, I would have some worries. If it was against some of the so-called Christian institutions, I would have even greater worries. But thank God, it is not against us! It is against the Lord and against His anointed, so we know who is going to win.

Yet I have set my king, Upon my holy hill of Zion

Let us move on a little further and see for a moment the purpose of the Lord that we have here revealed in this second Psalm. It is really very wonderful, because we have three things revealed in this Psalm which constitute the eternal purpose of God. The heart of this whole conflict, all the battle that rages, is over this purpose of the Lord. In verse six we have two things and in verse eight we have the third. First is the King, the second is Zion, the mountain of My holiness, and third is the uttermost parts of the earth for thy possession. Here we have three glorious things which constitute the eternal purpose of God.

The King

Right from the very beginning the Son was destined to be heir of the world. If we believe the Book, it says that Satan came and said,

"I will be like the Most High. I will exalt my throne above the stars of God" (see Isaiah 14:13–14). In other words, if I do not misread the Word, it is as if Satan was jealous of the Lord Jesus and jealous of the purpose of the Father for the Son and said, "*I* will take His place. *I* will be exalted. *I* will set my throne above all."

The whole of human history is really the expression of this battle over the divinely foreordained King. He is the anointed One. We have it here in these wonderful words: "... against the Lord and against His anointed." Anointed. You know the King was an anointed person. Of course, you have to understand a little bit about the Old Testament and about Jewish things to understand that this is the Messiah King, sometimes called the Messianic King, the Messiah Redeemer King, the Messiah King. Whenever you see the word *anointed* you immediately must think in English, *the Messiah King*. This was the One who was waited for and why those wise men came from far saying, "Where is He that is born, King of the Jews, for we have seen His star in the East" (Matthew 2:2). The King.

It is the most wonderful thing as far as I am concerned to understand this because it goes to the heart of the whole. I begin to understand why from the very moment that God gave that promise to Eve, Satan raged. He raged! You remember, the Lord said to the serpent, "Upon thy belly shalt thou go, and dust shalt thou eat." Then He said, "He shall bruise thy head, and you shall bruise his heel" (Genesis 3:14–15). From that moment the conflict began.

In this context, listen to this very well-known verse in Ephesians 1:9–10: "Making known unto us the mystery of His will according to His good pleasure, which He purposed in Him," (that is in Jesus) "unto a dispensation unto the fulness of the times, to sum up, or head up, all things in Christ, things in the heavens and things upon the earth." So here you have the purpose of the Lord. It is to have the King and to head up everything in heaven and on earth in that King. So that is what the whole occasion of the storm is over.

Now, listen dear believer. If you are wondering what on earth we have been talking about, just listen to this. The battle in your life may largely be over the question of who is Lord in your life. What is going on in your life? Sometimes this sense of civil war, this sense of inner dissension, this sense of everything going wrong, may well be a cameo of something else in the world because you have not settled the question of the lordship of Jesus. Until you and I really settle this question of the lordship of Jesus, we will never get anywhere. There is no real lasting joy, no real lasting peace, no real abundant life, there is no permanent being filled with the Spirit, no anointing of the Spirit that goes on and on and on unless you and I have really bowed the knee to the Lord Jesus as Lord, as well as received Him as Saviour. There is nothing more miserable than a life that is saved and not under the lordship of its Saviour. Yet thousands of us live these lives, don't we? I know believers who spent 20 years of their Christian life arguing with the Lord. At the very end, they throw in the glove when there is nothing else worth having and finally give in to the Lord. Then comes the joy and the peace and they say, "Oh, what a fool I've been! For twenty years I've thrown away my life!"

It is the same with church life. I could take you to place after place where He is not Lord. He is proclaimed as Saviour, but He is not Lord. The leaders, the responsible people, do not know how to bow the knee to the Lord. They do not know how to find the mind of the Lord. They do not know how to detect and define the mind of the Lord and they do not even know how to do the mind of the Lord. Some people actually say that we have been given common sense; we ought not to go and ask the Lord for such things. This common-sense leads the Lord's people into the most fearful death I have ever seen because they all put their heads together instead of really seeking to know Him.

Let me put it this way. When you really begin to know how to know the mind of the Lord, you have to use your head. It requires quite a lot of "head using" under the government of the Spirit to really know the mind of the Lord. Some people like to be little passive nothings, sort of sitting there for some revelation to come, as if that is how guidance comes. Guidance doesn't come like that. It can be very dangerous. It is what the Oxford movement did, empty your head and wait for something to come in. Well, sometimes it can come from a wrong source. No, no, no, we have to have a renewed mind. Not an old mind, but a renewed mind so that we can read the mind of the Lord, understand the will of the Lord, and be enabled to do it.

Now, don't you think this is rather wonderful that He is going to head up all things in the heavens and on earth in the Lord Jesus? Now that is what the battle is over! So, dear friend, why don't you settle it in your life now? What a wonderful way to start these times together! Far from being dull and dreary and life-sapping, they will become absolutely like a revival to you. Suddenly you wake up and think, "Oh, my goodness! He has been talking about this battle raging over the purpose of the Lord and now I suddenly realise that is what's been happening in my little life. I have never settled this issue with the Lord. The whole battle is over the King!"

Oh, how gracious the Lord is to save us! I think of myself when the Lord saved me. He loved me so much that He was prepared to save me even though I would not take Him as Lord. Isn't it so with you? The Lord loves us so much that like Israel of old, He will do anything that He may save us. Then He will let us play around and muck around and waste opportunities and destroy the whole usefulness and value of our lives until in the end He's only got the debris. Still, He will save the debris, but do you want it to be like that? As sure as I stand here tonight, some of you young people, if the Lord tarries 20 years' time, your lives will have been valueless. If you say to me, "Why?" I will tell you why. Because today you did not settle the issue of the lordship of Jesus. There is no other way to be happy in the Lord than to trust and obey. You cannot trust the Lord if you have not made Him Lord. When you think you have a better head on you than He has on Him, you will trust yourselves not Him. When you think that you have a better idea of what is good for you than He has, you are going to have a fight with Him. But if you know His lordship, you will trust Him, and you will obey Him. You will discover the most wonderful thing: that He loves you so much, He will become your guardian and protector and provider and educator and trainer and everything you need.

Royal Character

Now, come back to it: the King, the anointed One. This King is not only King in title and in pedigree, He is King in character. That is all so wonderful, isn't it? He is the King in character. This one is not there because He has got a title in front of Him, because He was born King of the Jews, because He had a marvellous pedigree that goes right back through the royal house of David, then back to Abraham. Do you know why He is King? It is because He proved that He has got royal character, that's why. When did He prove that He had royal character? In three years of public ministry when He endured the gainsaying of sinners, when He was at the service of all and sundry, night and day. What an amazing story it is! Forgive it if I say it again, but I always say that He proved His worthiness to be King when what we call the mystique of royalty was stripped from Him. When He was stripped naked, beaten black and blue, His beard pulled out in tufts, spittle all over His face, eyes swollen, dressed up in an officer's purple cloak, a crown of thorns jammed on His head, a reed placed in His hands, and coarse soldiers playing a game with Him. There, when He lost all that we would call the mystique of royalty, the kingliness of Jesus shines. Those soldiers had no idea what they were doing when they said, "Hail, King of the Jews." It was mockery on their part, but the whole of heaven was on its knees, prostrate in worship. God had found the One who was worthy to be King—not only foreordained King, not only with a pedigree that was absolutely pure, not only with a title as far as God is concerned, but He had the character. King.

That is what the battle is all over, you know? It is not just over the lordship of Jesus in your life, it is the producing of kingliness. If you like, you ladies, since we live in the day of women's lib: 'queenliness,' but you know what I mean. Something is being produced in your life which means you can do no other than reign. Now I say, that is something worth having. If I am going to be in a battle, I don't mind it, if in this battle God is producing a quality in me, a value in me, and a character in me which is going to come to the throne. I do not mind it. You surely won't mind the kitchen sink, or the factory bench, or the school, or the hospital, or the humdrum, if we at least know that somehow through it all God is doing something.

Our Lord spent 30 years, more or less, at a carpenter's bench. It must have been so routine, so humdrum. Can you imagine those dear people coming with their complaints about how 'this wasn't right' or 'that wasn't right' or 'this wasn't made accordingly,' when of course He knew very well He had done exactly what He had been asked to do. He was the carpenter of the whole place. Then He had three years of public ministry. Anyone who knows anything about public ministry knows how irritating people can be! It is a source of continual condemnation to me when I think of how the Lord dealt with people, and crowds of people, knowing how short tempered one gets. You are all human; you know exactly what it means. Unless you are very naïve and gullible, crowds are very irritating. They don't listen and then as soon as you have shut up, they ask you a question on what you just said. Then you feel like boxing their ears, you know? But not the Lord! I am sure the Lord was firm and strong and clear and truthful. But oh, the patience of the Lord!

That is why when we come to the book of Revelation, we find that the Lion of Judah, the little lamb as it has been slain, is in the midst of the throne and the whole of the creation, angelic and human, the whole creation is on its knees in worship before Him. They sing this song, "Worthy is the Lamb that was slain to have the power and the dominion and the glory Revelation 5:12

and so on. Well, of course, He is not just there because He has got a pedigree or because He has got a title. God preserve us from ever getting this mentality, this kind of ambition: "I want a position, I want a title, I want a status in the Church, I want to be something!" May the Lord help us.

God never wants to produce an eternal civil service, well, not like the one down here. Forgive me all civil servants, but you know what I mean—empty-headed people who just go by a book and believe in red tape ... and more of it. God preserve us! We don't want that kind of eternity, do we? We want people occupying position who have got character, who have got the same lamb-like character as the King, the same quality of compassion, the same quality of sensitiveness, the same inwrought capacity for understanding men and women. Above all, they understand the will and mind of God. That can only come in walking with the King. Well, here you have got it; there is the King.

Zion

We are going to take up the next two things at a later time. What I am going to do now is just underline them. I will leave them with you so that you can take away this Psalm, really pray about it, and study it. The first thing is: the "King." The King is everything as far as God is concerned—everything. The second thing is "My holy hill of Zion." We will talk about that next time. My version says, "Yet have I set my king upon My holy hill of Zion." (I do not know why it puts it like that in this version. It is normally quite good.) Really, literally, it is: "Yet, have I set My king upon Zion, the mountain of My holiness." Of course, this is just like Psalm 48:1 where it speaks of the mountain of His holiness.

Well, you see all this means *Zion*. I suppose some of you youngsters, the only thing you ever think of with Zion is one of those dear old Welsh chapels, you know, grey stone and carved on the outside "Zion."

It is interesting, really, this whole word *Zion*, but next time we will see that the word Zion takes a very large portion of the Bible. Once we really start to read all the various times Zion is mentioned and in what connection, it is quite incredible! This thing about Zion has tremendous importance. You will remember that the Lord said in Psalm 132:13–14, sometimes we sing those words together, "For the Lord hath chosen Zion; He hath desired it for His habitation. This is My resting-place for ever: Here will I dwell; for I have desired it."

Now, is it not incumbent upon us to begin to ask the Lord, "What is this Zion?" The Lord has chosen it. He has desired it for His habitation and that old word means His home. If He has desired it for His dwelling place, here will I dwell forever, surely we ought to find out what it is all about! What does it mean?

When we come back to Psalm 2, we find this is the heart of the conflict. It is not, "I have set My King at My right hand." It is, "Yet have I set My King upon Zion, the mountain of My Holiness." In other words, the Lord has a purpose for this King which is not just to do with the invisible and with the heavenly. It has somehow a connection with the earth and this Zion is something that you and I are in.

Do you remember the word in Psalm 84:5: "In whose hearts are the highways to Zion"? In some of the modern versions they have dropped out Zion because it is not in the original. However, it is there because if you read on in the next few verses you see, "Every one of them appeareth before God in Zion." So, the highways are that we may appear in Zion before His face.

Now, have you got these highways? You see, I find a lot of believers have got no highways. They have no highways to Zion. They do not know where they are going. They know they are saved. They know they should witness. They know that they should do some good works. They know that they should read the Book. They know that they should do some good works and they should pray. But they do not know where they are going. But it is a wonderful thing to have the highways to Zion in one's heart and to be quite clear as to where God is leading us. We may not know the path between here and the end, but at least we know where we are going. It is clear. We know why the Lord is dealing with us, why He is leading us, and where He is leading us. The path that He may choose to take is His business. "The highways to Zion." What a wonderful comfort! This conflict is raging over the matter of the King being *in* His Zion. May the Lord help us.

You see, the writer of the Hebrew letter says, "Ye have come unto Mount Zion to the city of the living God," and the next moment he says, "We have no continuing city here, but we seek that which is to come" (Hebrews 12:22 and 13:14). In other words, you are there and you are not there. You have come, and you haven't. You are in, and you are not. That is what the battle is all over. Praise the Lord, we know who is going to win it!

That is why those wonderful chapters, Revelation 4 and 5, speak of the little Lamb, the Lion of Judah, in the midst of the throne and the whole creation bows before Him and sings that song: "Worthy is the Lamb that was slain Who has redeemed us to God by His blood out of every tongue, and kindred, and people, and nation." Then it says, "Unto Him be the glory and the dominion and the power forever." Then, when you go on you come to all these beasts and dragons and false prophets and I don't know what else, but at the end—at the end, you come to a city. That city comes down to the earth out of heaven having the glory of God. There is something about that city. It is connected with the throne and with the King. It says the throne of the Lord God, the Almighty and of the Lamb art therein; and it says that His servants, or bondslaves, shall serve Him. They shall see His face and they shall reign forever and ever. That is something wonderful as far as I am concerned. It thrills me because it means that in this whole battle we are in, the enemy cannot "unsave" us. He cannot bring us to the place where we lose our salvation. However, he can bring us to the place where we are disqualified as far as the city is concerned. May God help us. What a battle!

The Uttermost Parts of the Earth for Thy Possession

Lastly, of course, there is dominion. In this Psalm 2:8 it says, "Ask of Me and I will give thee the nations for thine inheritance and the uttermost parts of the earth for thy possession." Uttermost parts of the earth for thy possession. Nations for thine inheritance. What is this? It is dominion. You have the King, you have Zion, and you have the uttermost parts of the earth for His possession, the nations for His inheritance. You have it all there. It is the purpose of God. "The earth is the Lord's and the fulness thereof. The world and they that dwell therein." But how? That is the point, isn't it? That is what the battle is over. The battle is over whether or not the people of God will take their place with the King—down here on earth—to execute the will of God, to see that those nations, the uttermost parts of the earth, become His inheritance. It is one thing to say, "Well, if the Lord is there, why doesn't He just ask for China? He'll get it." My dear friends, as a dear older sister dear Momma Hurley used to say, who is now lying ill in her last days in West Middlesex, "That old hymn says, 'Waft, waft ye winds, the story ...'" She said, "The winds have never wafted the story! It has taken two hands, two feet, a human mouth, and a human heart."

Now you come back to kingship. Unless the Lord gets His position in your life and my life, in our life together as the people of God, how can we be so identified with Him that we can do His will? When He says "Go," we go. When He says, "Come," we come. If He tells us to go to the ends of the earth we will go to the ends of the earth. If He tells us to remain, we will remain, but we are under His government and we are together in this thing. It is a Zion. It is not just something individual. It is not just moving out here and there as we think, as I think, as you think, without any relation to Him, but we are a Zion. The King is in His Zion and He is able to manifest His mind. We test it out together and we do the will of God.

Oh, wouldn't it be wonderful if we could at least gain the ascendancy spiritually? If we could only take the place that we ought to take in the unseen as far as one area is concerned and perhaps the Lord would lead us in the end for whole countries! We have had so many promises now and in the earlier days about the Thames Valley. Now my dear friends, we cannot just sit here like little passive nothings and say, "One day the Lord will do it. One day the Lord will do it because He said it." We have to cooperate with the Lord. There is a battle to be fought and to be won because we know the will of God. There is His mind actually to be carried into practice.

It is tremendous, is it not? I think it is. When I looked at this, I thought, "How wonderful it is, here we have the purpose of the Lord, three things: the King, Zion the mountain of His holiness, and the uttermost parts of the earth for His possession." Dear child of God, that is what the battle is over. If you are feeling it, and if I am feeling it, and if we are feeling it together, praise the Lord, we are in a good apostolic succession. This is a battle that goes right back to the beginning and we expect to see it get infinitely more fiery and ferocious before the King comes. But oh, the joy when finally the King does come!

May the Lord help us then in this matter because the Lord has very simply said, "Yet, have I set, My King upon Zion, the mountain of My holiness." He is not going to be shaken. That is His declared intent and the King is going to remain there. The question is whether you and I will be in it. May God give us grace to be found right there with Him.

Shall we pray?

Well, Lord, Thou hast heard all this that we have talked about and there is a lot in it, Lord. But we need Thy help. We pray Lord, would Thou be so gracious to us that, Lord, it would come to us with divine illumination and divine revelation. We pray, Lord, that even the oldest amongst us may receive from Thee through this little time. Lord, would Thou continue with us? Oh, Lord, will Thou really begin to write some practical things on our hearts as we start to deal with some of those things. Lord, hear us and give us what we need—a marvellous, double portion of Thy Spirit. We ask it in the name of our Lord Jesus. Amen.

2.
The Building of Zion

Isaiah 61:1–62:2

The Spirit of the Lord God is upon me; because the Lord hath anointed me to preach good tidings unto the meek; he hath sent me to bind up the broken-hearted, to proclaim liberty to the captives, and the opening of the prison to them that are bound; to proclaim the year of the Lord's favour, and the day of vengeance of our God; to comfort all that mourn; to appoint unto them that mourn in Zion, to give unto them a garland for ashes, the oil of joy for mourning, the garment of praise for the spirit of heaviness; that they may be called trees of righteousness, the planting of the Lord, that he may be glorified. And they shall build the old wastes, they shall raise up the former desolations, and they shall repair the waste cities, the desolations of many generations. And strangers shall stand and feed your flocks, and foreigners shall be your ploughmen and your vine-dressers. But ye shall be named the priests of the Lord; men shall call you the ministers of our

God: ye shall eat the wealth of the nations, and in their glory shall ye boast yourselves. Instead of your shame ye shall have double; and instead of dishonor they shall rejoice in their portion: therefore in their land they shall possess double; everlasting joy shall be unto them. For I, the Lord, love justice, I hate robbery with iniquity; and I will give them their recompense in truth, and I will make an everlasting covenant with them. And their seed shall be known among the nations, and their offspring among the peoples; all that see them shall acknowledge them, that they are the seed which the Lord hath blessed.

I will greatly rejoice in the Lord, my soul shall be joyful in my God; for he hath clothed me with the garments of salvation,

he hath covered me with the robe of righteousness, as a bridegroom decketh himself with a garland, and as a bride adorneth herself with her jewels. For as the earth bringeth forth its bud, and as the garden causeth the things that are sown in it to spring forth; so the Lord God will cause righteousness and praise to spring forth before all the nations.

For Zion's sake will I not hold my peace, and for Jerusalem's sake I will not rest, until her righteousness go forth as brightness, and her salvation as a lamp that burneth. And the nations shall see thy righteousness, and all kings thy glory, and thou shalt be called by a new name, which the mouth of the Lord shall name.

The little phrase that I have taken as the theme for these times is in Isaiah 62:1, "For Zion's sake will I not hold my peace, and for

Jerusalem's sake I will not rest, until her righteousness go forth as brightness, and her salvation as a lamp that burneth." For Zion's sake. Last time I shared on the second Psalm and particularly underlined that wonderful little verse six in that Psalm, "Yet have I set my King upon Zion, the mountain of My holiness." Then it goes on, "I will tell of the decree: This day have I begotten Thee. Ask of Me, and I will give thee the nations for thine inheritance, and the uttermost parts of the earth for thy possession."

What is Zion?

I want to take the little word *Zion* and ask a question. What really is this *Zion*? It is in fact spoken about again, and again, and again in the Word. For instance, in Isaiah 60:14, we read these wonderful words, these prophetic words, "And the sons of them that afflicted thee shall come bending unto thee; and all they that despised thee shall bow themselves down at the soles of thy feet; and they shall call thee the city of the Lord, the Zion of the Holy One of Israel." They shall call thee, the city of the Lord, the Zion, of the Holy One of Israel. The *Zion* of the Holy One of Israel. That is what the Word of the Lord says the redeemed of the Lord shall be called. What is Zion? There are few names which are mentioned more in the Bible than this name Zion. I also suppose there are few names that are probably more misunderstood.

I am sure that some of you younger folks probably associate Zion with strange old Victorian hymns. *Marching to Zion* is a good one, written by Isaac Watts, and come to think of it, I think that it is probably a little older than the Victorian era, but in the way we sing it, it is in fact more like a mid-nineteenth century hymn.

Many people's idea of Zion is some little grey stone chapel in Wales, with the word *Zion* engraved above the door. Or sometimes you find it round these parts, normally small chapels belonging to a particular denomination, and they are called *Zion*.

The Bible has a tremendous amount to say about Zion. These are just a few.

We read:

of Mount Zion

of the stronghold of Zion

of Zion the city of the great King

of the inhabitants of Zion

of the daughter of Zion

of the *daughters* of Zion

of the children of Zion

We are told:

that the Lord loves the gates of Zion

that He has founded Zion

that He calls it "My holy hill of Zion"

that He has chosen Zion

that He dwells in Zion

that He is great in Zion

that He fights for Zion

that He is jealous for Zion

that He will roar from Zion

that out of Zion, the perfection of beauty, He hath shined forth

that the Redeemer will come to Zion

that He will save Zion

that He will build Zion

that He will comfort Zion

that He will reign in Zion

that ... *the ransomed of the Lord shall return, and come with singing unto Zion; and everlasting joy shall be upon their heads: they shall obtain gladness and joy; and sorrow and sighing shall flee away.*

Now, that is only a little sample of the way this term or name Zion is used in Scripture, but I hope it is enough for you to realise that we are dealing with a vitally important matter. We are not dealing with some little side-line of the Bible, some little side-path of the Bible. We are dealing with something that God speaks of in association with Himself. He speaks of it as something that He loves, as something that He saves, something that He dwells in, something that He has chosen, something that means a tremendous amount to Him. He speaks of it as something from which we can depart and something to which we can return. It is very important therefore that we should understand just what this is all about, don't you think? However young we are in the Lord, or however old we are in the Lord, here is a matter upon which we need the Lord to pour divine illumination.

Now if you are young in the Lord, and you almost feel like switching off at the very thought of talking about Zion because it seems a bit old-fashioned somehow, don't switch off! Instead, just ask the Lord to really give to you an original, your *own* original understanding of this matter. Something that the older ones may not quite see as you see, but in a way that you may see it for *yourself*. I don't mean that you see it in an entirely different way than the older ones, but you see it for yourself. When you see something for yourself, it changes your life! When you really begin to see it for yourself, suddenly the importance of it and its fundamental nature dawns on you. So, ask the Lord even now in the quietness of your heart, "Lord, will you meet me in this matter, and really give me an understanding of what this subject is about, what this name Zion is?"

The Use of "Zion" in Scripture

Now, the name Zion is used four ways in the Scripture. It is a very interesting thing that in Hebrew, after all the years of study there has been on this subject, we cannot yet actually discover the real meaning of the name Zion. In Hebrew it is *siyôn*. We just cannot find the meaning; we do not know. It has been suggested that it comes from the word which means "a dry, parched up ground." Well, that is very interesting if it does mean that, isn't it, that the Lord should have chosen a dry, parched up ground? It is certainly true of Jerusalem. Jerusalem is the only capital city in the world that was chosen without its own fountain or spring of water within its gates. The little spring of Gihon was always outside until dear Hezekiah got the idea from the Lord that he should blast away, as it were, through solid rock for 1,777 feet and bring the spring of Gihon right inside the city walls. Yet, until that time it must have been the only capital city in the world that was selected as a capital and did not have its own water supply within its walls!

Well, it may be that this is just what the Lord has done, just as Zion or Jerusalem is a smaller hill surrounded by higher mountains. There is not a single mountain around Jerusalem that is not higher than those three little, smaller mountains, hills that have been chosen for the site of Jerusalem. That was again because the Lord did not want them to have a high place. He did not want them to have a high place like the rest of the nations in which they would worship. So, He chose the three hills that were a little lower than the surrounding mountains that are round about Jerusalem.

In the same way maybe, He chose it as a dried up, parched ground deliberately so that, as the Psalmist says, "all my springs are in thee." There is another suggestion made more recently by Jewish scholars that says that *Zion* really comes from a word which means *stronghold* or *rock*. Well, we do not know, but there are four ways in which the word Zion is used in Scripture.

Mount Zion

First of all, it is used as an *actual geographical mountain* or hill called Mount Zion upon which Jerusalem is built. Psalm 78:68 says, "But God chose the tribe of Judah, the Mount Zion which He loved." You have it again of course in Psalm 48:2, "Beautiful in elevation, the joy of the whole earth is Mount Zion." So, it is an actual geographical mountain or hill in the promised land. That is the first way it is used in Scripture.

By the way, as a side point, it is almost certain that Mount Zion is to be identified in its beginnings with Mount Moriah and Mount Ophel. It was not independent of them as it is today. In other words, for those of you who know a little of Jerusalem, the southwestern hill which is today called Mount Zion only came to be called Mount Zion from the time of King Hezekiah. Before then, it was probable that Mount Moriah, upon which the temple was built, was Mount Zion. So, Mount Moriah, Mount Ophel, the Jebusite city, were really Mount Zion to begin with. This clears up a number of problems in the Word about the temple being on Mount Zion and so on. Later as the city spread, the West End (as we would call it) of the city, the upper-class part of the city, took the name Mount Zion for themselves.

Zion, the City of God

The second way this word Zion is used, is of the *city of God*. It is not just a mountain, or a hill, but it is a name for the city of God, for Jerusalem. It is synonymous with Jerusalem. If you look at II Samuel 5:7, you read: "Nevertheless, David took the stronghold of Zion; the same is the city of David." Then again in Psalm 48:1–2: "Great is the Lord, and greatly to be praised, in the city of our God, in His holy mountain, beautiful in elevation, the joy of the whole earth, is mount Zion, on the sides of the north, the city of the great King." Then again, you find in verses 12–13: "Walk about Zion, go round about her, number the towers thereof; mark ye well her bulwarks; consider her palaces." In other words, the name Zion is not just a mountain. It has become the name for the city of God, for Jerusalem. Again, that is how it is used.

Zionism, a Movement

Then, it is used (and this is not often understood) in a third way in Scripture. I want to make this perfectly clear. I believe in it with all my heart that it is used for that national and political movement, which we call *Zionism*. Now this is where a point of controversy immediately comes because there are those who say, "How on earth can a national and political movement for the liberation of the Jewish people, led by agnostics and in some cases atheists, be predicted in the Word of God or found in the Word of God?" Yet it is. Now, I am not going to dwell on it. If we really believe that the re-creation of the state of Israel is the fulfillment of God's prophetic word and the hand of God is behind it, we cannot discount or ignore that political, national movement by which it came into being.

We read for instance in Psalm 137:1–6 those very wonderful words, which I believe are in connection with this: "By the rivers of Babylon, there we sat down, yea, we wept, when we remembered Zion. Upon the willows in the midst thereof we hanged up our harps. For there they that led us captive required of us songs, and they that wasted us required of us mirth, saying, Sing us one of the songs of Zion. How shall we sing the Lord's song in a foreign land? If I forget thee, O Jerusalem, let my right hand forget her skill. Let my tongue cleave to the roof of my mouth, if I remember thee not; if I prefer not Jerusalem above my chief joy."

Now, I would like to know what value this Psalm has in the book. I mean—what is it? Is it just the fossilised sorrow of the people of God in the first exile? Is that all the meaning of it? If there are those who see in this Psalm something of the travail of heart of those who know the Lord and love the Lord and who sorrow over the state of the people of God, over the church of God, over the Body of the Lord Jesus, then I can see some value in this Psalm. But I cannot believe that God just puts antiques in His Word, just things that are sort-of fossilised points of history, that we can see in this Psalm, something that meant a lot to people 2,600 years ago, but has absolutely no bearing whatsoever upon us today. I cannot believe it. No, I think that it is the expression of that desire of God's earthly people to really know a renewing of their sovereignty as a state amongst the states of the earth.

Of course, if you turn to Jeremiah, you will find this again in a way that cannot, I think, really be denied. In Jeremiah 30:11, the Lord says, "For I am with thee, saith the Lord, to save thee," [that is of Israel], "for I will make a full end of all the nations whither I have scattered thee, but I will not make a full end of thee; but I will correct thee in measure, and will in no wise leave thee unpunished." Verse 17, "For I will restore health unto thee, and I will heal thee of thy wounds, saith the Lord; because they have called thee an outcast, saying, It is Zion, for whom no one cares, or no one seeks." Well, that again, I think, is to be related to the physical side of things, for there is a literal meaning to some of these prophecies.

One last one for you is Isaiah 66:8, "Who hath heard such a thing? who hath seen such things? Shall a land be born in one day? Shall a nation be brought forth at once?" Now how do you spiritualise that, may I ask? If we say that this is the church, we cannot say she was brought forth at once. Then it goes on, "For as soon as Zion travailed, she brought forth her children." There were 1,800 years of Jewish anguish and sorrow, in which they were dispersed to the ends of the earth and took it lying down, believing that it was the judgment and curse of God upon them. No Jewish bride would wear gold or silver on her wedding gown because of it. Every Jewish man who built a home left a little portion near the door unfinished to remind him that they had lost Zion. They were never allowed to play orchestral music except on special and specified occasions. All these regulations were to remind the people they had lost their beloved Zion. It had been taken from them because of transgression.

What is interesting is this: that literally at the end of the last century in 1897 (really that is when it began), there came into being a movement called *Zionism*. The moment Zionism came into being and began to travail, within 50 short years she brought forth her sons and after 1,900 years of exile and sorrow, in 50 years the thing was done. It was the most anguished period of Jewish history, but in the end, a land was born in one single day, the 14th of May 1948. A nation was brought forth at once. Now, we must not spend too much time on this matter, but you see that is a third point. It goes through scriptures and those who ignore it or try to overlook it are going to come into very real problems in the last days because this matter is really a vital indication of where we are in the economy of God.

The Eternal and Spiritual Zion

Of course, the fourth way Zion is used is the eternal and the spiritual. This is the most important thing of all. It is that matter which has been on the heart of God and in the mind of God from before times eternal. It is that which He had longed for and that which He conceived when He created the universe and created man and woman. It was something that was in His heart from the very beginning. He called it Zion. That is how it came to be called later: Zion. It is more than an ideal. It is the very expression of the desire and longing and purpose of God for mankind.

You have it for instance, in Psalm 50:1–2, "The Mighty One, God, the Lord, hath spoken, and called the earth from the rising of the sun unto the going down thereof. Out of Zion, the perfection of beauty, God hath shined forth." Now, I know Jerusalem and Zion, probably as well as anybody, and I must say this: both from the historical point of view and from the contemporary point of view, I do not think that Jerusalem has ever been the perfection of beauty. I can understand some people going and being disappointed by it. They have these Sunday School notions of some wonderful, great city of gold and silver and all the rest of it—so clean, so pure, so holy, the perfection of beauty,

God shining out of it; what they see are smelly old bazaars and souks, flea-bitten alleys and smelly sewers, baksheesh everywhere and a lot of other things! Of course, if that is all they see, I am very sorry for them because you should be able to see beyond that—to what it symbolises and of what it is—an expression.

This expression of beauty is the eternal and spiritual Zion which has been on the heart of God from the beginning. When we turn to Hebrews 12:22 we read those wonderful words: "But ye are come unto Mount Zion, unto the city of the living God, and unto the heavenly Jerusalem, and to innumerable hosts of angels." You have come to Mount Zion, to the city of the living God, the heavenly Jerusalem. This is the fourth way that this word Zion is used in Scripture.

God's Desire

Having said that, let us look a little more closely at this whole matter. What is this Zion of the Holy One of Israel that we read of in Isaiah 60:12? Well, as I have said, it is that which really is in the very heart of God for us from the beginning. Previously we read Psalm 132:13–14: "For the Lord hath chosen Zion; He hath desired it for his habitation. This is my resting-place for ever: here will I dwell; for I have desired it." Now these are incredible words. Have they ever really sunk into you? Listen again to what the Lord says here, "The Lord has chosen Zion. He has desired it for His home." Did you get that? He has chosen Zion. He has desired it for His home! When a person goes out to look for a house, for a home, they have got to have a *house* to have a *home*. However, you can have a *house* without a *home*. Yet when you have got the two together you have got a great boon and blessing. When a person looks for a house, for a home, they know what they are looking for and when they find it, they say, "That's it. We choose it." Providing you have got plenty of money, you can buy what you have chosen. You have desired it for your home. You choose it. Now the Bible, the Word of God says that God has chosen Zion and desired it for His house, for His home, for His dwelling place, for His habitation. Does that begin to get into your heart?

You see, in one way, the thing is that we can only talk in Sunday School language. Thanks be to God, the Bible is in Sunday School language in one way, otherwise, half the world would never be able to understand it! Some people say, "Why isn't it more scientific?" Well, suppose it had been more scientific; we would only have those scientific nuts who would be able to understand it. People like myself would be tied up in knots! How would you ever unravel it if it was put in scientific terms? For century after century, and for very large parts of the earth, the Book would be completely impossible of any real understanding.

God has taken spiritual realities and expressed them in the simplest of human language. He has taken things like marriage and said, "Now, this is the illustration of what I want." He has taken a home and said, "This is what I want—not a bad home; I want a good home, all that a real home is meant to express. That is what I want." He says, "I want the union between a man and a woman which ends, not only in a home, but in a family and in service. This," God says, "is what I want. I don't want to be alone."

That is why the Lord Jesus says in one of those wonderful Messianic Psalms and quoted in Hebrews 2:12–13, "In the midst of the congregation ... I, and the children whom God has given me." What a wonderful little word! You know, you are the children. It says, "In the midst of the congregation ..." Actually in the Hebrew it is the word we use today for church: "In the midst of the great church I will praise Thy name." Then as He says in the book of Hebrews a little later, "I and the children whom God hath given me." It is as if the Lord says, "I don't want to be alone. I have come to glory." When He was transfigured in glory He could have stepped into the kingdom, but there would have been only one man in the kingdom. It would have been the Lord Jesus. Instead, He came back to the cross to die for us and was raised on the third day, so that He might save you and me and bring many sons unto glory with Him, so that He could share His glory, so that He could share His inheritance, His heritage, so that He could share His throne.

That, to me, makes a lot of sense and adds another dimension to the gospel. We are so used to hearing a gospel that is just to do with forgiveness of sins, just to do with being saved in that way—we get forgiveness of sins and then we become Christians— we forget that the gospel in this Book has more parts to it than that. It is not only a question of being forgiven, it is a question of being brought into union with Him. It is not only a question of being in union with Him, it is the question of being anointed with the Holy Spirit. It is not only a question of being anointed with the Holy Spirit, it is a question of becoming His Zion, so that we become His bride, so that we become the wife of the Lamb, so that we become the city of God, the New Jerusalem, the heavenly Jerusalem, so that we become His home, His dwelling place, the temple of the Lord. Oh, these terms, they spill out one after another!

If you think God is going to one day have an actual temple, you have got another thing coming. If you think that God is going to actually marry somebody, a lady called His wife, you have got another thing coming. Do you understand? In other words, what God has done is He has taken very simple ideas that you and I understand, and He has said, "Now, this is what I desire. This is what I long for. It is something like this in another dimension. It is something like this, not on the earth, but in the heavenly, not in the transient, but forever." A human home is only till death breaks it up. Marriage is only till death breaks it up. All these relationships down here are till death dissolves them, but the family of God, and the Zion of God, and the home of God, the household of faith—that is forever. Those are eternal relationships. That is a home and a family that lasts forever.

"My Resting Place"

Now, you come back to this wonderful matter and you begin to understand a little bit more about what the Psalmist was talking about: "The Lord hath chosen Zion, He hath desired it for His habitation. This is My resting place forever. Here will I dwell." Isn't it a wonderful thing to have a resting place? There is a vast difference between a hotel bedroom and a real resting place. I know something about this. I get shoved into beds of all sizes and shapes. Sometimes there is hardly a curtain at the window. There is only a bit of net. Sometimes there is not even that, just a shutter on the outside. If you're like me, I'm the kind of person that needs darkness to sleep, I find it terribly difficult. Then, you know, if you have got one of those little narrow, two-foot beds, I find it so hard on one of those. I feel as if I'm in a coffin. All night long, I am sort of afraid of, you know, expanding. It is not a resting place! It is just a lodgement. It is something to be endured. There is a vast difference between a resting place and a lodgement.

I feel sorry for anybody whose home is not a resting place. I know that one of the tragedies of contemporary life (and I suppose this has always been) is that homes, instead of being the place where you can rest, you can relax, you can be yourself, you can be absolutely truly what you are, become a place of tension, strain, artifice, and façade. Somehow or other people cannot really be themselves with one another, and cannot reach that sort of rock bottom level.

You see, a resting place has to be a place where you can be absolutely 100% yourself. That is the basis of relaxation. You cannot relax if you feel someone is studying you. Do you know what I mean? Well, of course, some people can; they are that kind of extrovert. They could relax right in front of anybody. However, if you feel that somehow or other someone is watching you, you don't feel like taking your corset off, or your wig off, or your false eyelashes off, or whatever else. You just don't feel like it when you are being studied, but if it is your home, you can be yourself. You can pad 'round in slippers. You can let your hair down. You can be yourself. I am not saying that it is always nice to sort of be totally yourself, but it is a resting place, isn't it?

Now, forget for one moment the coarser side of that and think of the Lord. "This is My resting place forever. Here will I dwell" (Psalm 132:14). He did not say, "Here will I visit," but, "Here will I dwell. This is My resting place." In other words, it is as if God is saying, "I long to be just absolutely Myself. Somewhere where I can share the secrets of My heart. Somewhere where I can open up the very inner secrets of My being."

That is why He refers to this in other places of the Bible as being like a marriage. He speaks of the church as being His bride, as being the wife of the Lamb. In another place He speaks of it as "growing into a holy temple in the Lord." It is interesting that it says in that final city there is no temple there. It says, "For the Lord God and the Lamb are the temple thereof." It is as if somehow, we in Him have become the temple of God in which there is eternal praise, eternal worship, eternal communion, and eternal service.

Union and Communion

It doesn't matter what terms you use to look on this thing, for instance, head and body. You have never seen a living, bodiless head; you have never seen a living, headless body, have you? The whole point of head and body is that they are stuck together. I mean, woe betide us if you and I get divided from our heads. We will not live very long, will we? The whole point of a head and a body is that they belong together and function together. They are part of a living, organic whole. Now, that is a term that is used again and again in the New Testament for this Zion: head and body. The Lord Jesus is the head, and the body as it were, is brought out of Him, produced out of His nature and life. You and I are members of the Lord Jesus and members one of another.

Or again, take the vine. Jesus said, "I am the true vine, and My Father is the husbandman" (John 15:1). Then He said, "Abide in Me and I in you as the branches cannot bear fruit except they abide in the vine, no more can ye except ye abide in Me" (John 15:4). Now, the wonderful thing is that all those dear disciples, being Jewish, when they heard the Lord say this they knew just what He was talking about. However, it was a great shock to them because, for them, they knew that the vine was Israel. It was the covenant people of God.

Josephus, that great historian of the first century, tells us that one of the incredible wonders of the ancient world was that great golden vine—out of gold, all tracery work, with great grapes and tendrils and leaves hanging, which was right over the porch of the sanctuary. When the children of Israel came in to have their rams, or bullocks, or turtle doves slain and offered on the altar, looking up they saw this amazing gold filigree work.

Now when Jesus said, "I am the true vine," it must have been a terrible shock to them. They might have said, "How can He be?" To say He is Messiah of the chosen people is one thing, or to say He is the King. Even if He said He was High Priest of the people of God they might have understood. If He had said, "I am the Leader of the people of God, or Saviour of the people," but how can He *be* the people of God? Yet the Lord Jesus said, "I am the true vine. Abide in Me and I in you!" He said, "I am the vine; you are the branches." Most people understand that as if He were saying, "I am the trunk; you are the branches." He didn't say, "I am the trunk; you are the branches." He said, "I am the vine; you are the branches." In other words, "I am *the whole thing*. I am the root, the trunk, the branches, the tendrils, the leaves, the blossom, and the fruit, and you are in Me! You are part of me. You have become partakers of Me. You are branches in Me! So, abide in Me and I in you."

You see it is the same thought again—Zion. The heart of this whole thing is union. Do you begin to see it now? It is union. Just like marriage is one man and one woman blending together, taking one name, living in one home, producing one family, sharing one life, with one purpose, so God has desired that He might bring *us* into such a relationship with Himself. We may be surnamed with His name. We may share His life. We may share His heritage. We may share in His purpose. There is so much to be able to say about this, but this begins somehow to unfold the whole matter of Zion to us, doesn't it?

If you turn to Psalm 87, you find something else which is very wonderful: "His foundation is in the holy mountains. The Lord loveth the gates of Zion more than all the dwellings of Jacob. Glorious things are spoken of thee, O city of God. [Or we could translate that: 'things of glory are spoken of thee, O city of God.'] I will make mention of Rahab and Babylon as among them that know me: Behold, Philistia, and Tyre, with Ethiopia: This one was born there" Psalm 87:1–4. Where? In Zion. "Yea, of Zion it shall be said, This one and that one was born in her; And the Most High himself will establish her. The Lord will count when He writeth up the peoples, This one was born there" (verses 5–6).

In other words, He says that if you are born of God, you are born in Zion. You may be Philistia, which is an old enemy of God's people, or Tyre, which was not, but was still not the people of God, or Rahab, which was Egypt, another great enemy of the people of God, or Ethiopia, which in the old days, a long, long way back was also an enemy of God. God says, "If you were born in these countries, but you are spiritually born of God, that is okay. Your birth there is cancelled out. You are registered in Zion." Now that means that every person in this room is a true Zionist. If you are born of God, you are a Zionist. You can be nothing else and you are in the greatest liberation movement the world has ever known. We are in the liberation movement of the Spirit of God to bring about the restoration of the whole earth to the Lord.

The King to Reign

So, we are back to Psalm 2: the King, Zion the mountain of His holiness, and the uttermost parts of the earth for His possession. That is the job of the church. You see, we do great injustice in this whole matter of Zion, for all we talk about is being built together, being built together, being built together. When we look at one another we think, "Oh, dear! Have I got to be built together?" We think, "What is the purpose of being built together? I am stuck here with So-and-So having to rub shoulders. Wouldn't it be easier to get out and do this, or fly out there and do this, or go over there and get on with the job?"

But my dear friend, the whole point of being built together is not to stop there. It is not just a factory for bad times, much as some would try to make it like that. You know, as if the whole point of being in Zion is to have bad times, and the more bad times you have, the better it really is. That is not the point of being in Zion. Our point of being in Zion is that being built together, growing together up into Him as head, fitly framed together in Him, we should be able to wield His authority. We should start, as it were, to reign now over the nations. We should start to command the will of God to be done concerning this matter and that matter and the other matter. But we cannot do it unless we are built together, unless we begin to learn to find each other in the Lord, unless we learn to know what it is to be fitly framed together, knit together. Until there is something of that process taking place, there cannot be the authority of the Lord going out of Zion, so that as it says in Psalm 110:2, "The Lord will send forth the rod of thy strength out of Zion: rule thou in the midst of thine enemies."

Don't you see that the King wants to rule in the midst of His enemies in Richmond? Don't you see that the King wants to rule in the midst of His enemies in Britain? Don't you see that He longs to send forth the rod of His strength out of Zion? If there is no Zion what shall He do? If you opt-out, and someone else opts out, and someone else opts out, after a while, our authority in prayer will diminish and diminish and diminish. "Well," someone says, "I don't know what all this talk is about having to find each other in the Lord and having to be built together. What is it all about?" Then the enemy whispers to you and says, "Well, of course they're a bit queer anyway. You know, take the good and leave the bad." After a while of course, our authority in prayer will diminish and we will just become so many little prayer meetings—that's all— praying about so many little petitions. Only God can burn this thing into our hearts in such a way that we begin to see.

Now you younger ones, there will come a time when some of you who are teenagers are going to have to take the whole thing on your own shoulders. God preserve us if when that day comes you are not ready for it. Oh, that you would start here and now to get to know the Lord and get to know things like this and allow

God to bring you into the house of God and find your place! Of course you say straightaway, "Oh dear, some of those old ones, they would kill me!" I don't know whether it would kill you; I think it might even release you. I tell you one thing–you would probably do them a world of good. There is nothing like a few young ones really coming in with a fresh contribution and some originality to start sort of chivvying up all the old ones. I am not talking about just the old ladies, I mean all of us. We all get so old-maidish as we go on, don't we? We know it all. We have heard it for years. We have got a phraseology and we know how to sort of fit in at the right place. It is a wonderful thing when a few youngsters come in and start tripping across the traces. Everyone has to start waking up again. When you are told that someone cannot make head nor tail of your phraseology and suddenly you have to think again, "Well, what *do* we mean?"

You see, the real thing of this Zion is not just a lovely idea or an ideal that is marvellous but impossible in realisation. This is something that God wants to do down here amongst us on this earth! If it is not done here, dear ones, it will never be done up there.

So, do not cast away your confidence which has such great recompense of reward. Do not just throw in the glove and say, "Oh, dear, I feel weary with it all. I've heard this for years," and so on. Why not ask the Lord to breathe the whole thing into your heart in a new way, so that it becomes yours instead of second-hand through me or somebody else? It actually becomes yours and you begin to understand, "That's what it means. That's the heart. That's why the whole Bible talks about those things. This is what the Lord loves. This is what the Lord has chosen.

I want to be in that! I want to be part of that! When it speaks about Zion being built, compact together, I want to be in that! When it talks about the perfection of beauty, I want to be part of that perfection of beauty! When it talks about the rod of His strength going out, I want to know and experience that! When it talks about His ruling in the midst of His enemies, I want to know it!" Well, do you see what I mean when we talk about this?

The City

If you think that I am just talking out of the back of my head, look at Galatians 4:26: "But the Jerusalem that is above is free, which is our mother." Did you know you had a mother? I am not talking about the blessed virgin. Did you know that you have a mother? You have a mother. Your mother is the Zion which is above.

Then come back to what we mentioned before. Is it not important to have these highways to Zion in our hearts? It is one thing to have just a sort of cul-de-sacs. I think so many have got Christian cul-de-sacs. They have a Bible study and then it becomes a cul-de-sac, or just little prayer things on a local level, a personal level; it becomes a cul-de-sac. Some experience of the Holy Spirit, blessed and powerful as it is, becomes a cul-de-sac, or some experience of holiness can become a cul-de-sac.

Oh, to have the highways to Zion! There is only one thruway with God and that is Zion's highway. It is the only thruway. It is the only motorway of God. That is the way right through, the highway of God. Once you have got the highways to Zion in your heart you will never be the same again. If God were to give just a shaft of light into your heart, you will be spoiled for anything else for the rest of your life

Dear old Abraham ... people depict Abraham as if he were some smelly, illiterate, nomadic shepherd wandering around with a few scraggy goats and sheep. I have never heard of such nonsense in my life! Abraham was an aristocrat. Abraham came from a family of real standing in Ur of the Chaldees, a sophisticated city, one of the great centres of ancient civilisation. A lot of the ladies' jewellery is being copied from Ur of the Chaldees to this day. I don't know whether that is a good thing or a bad thing, but I am just saying that it is so. I mean, he was not anything so poor as people try to make out, as if God only had to whisper to Abraham and *whoosh*, he was out of that place like a bomb. Never! When Abraham went out of Ur of the Chaldees it was a colossal step of faith out of sophisticated civilisation into the desert. The only reason he did it was because he saw the city that has the foundations whose builder and architect is God. He had seen a city so tremendous, so eternal, with such foundations that Ur, with all its glory, was spoilt for him. He could never go back to it again.

That happens with you and me when we have really seen the city. May I just say this? Dear ones, we do not see the city as a thing. We see the city in God. Let me try to put it this way. You see, Stephen, before he was martyred said, "The God of glory appeared to our father Abraham and said, 'Get thee out of Ur of the Chaldees,'" (Acts 7:2–3). The writer to the Hebrews says that by faith Abraham obeyed to go out when he was called, not knowing whither he went (Hebrews 11:8). Then in verse ten he says, "For he looked for the city which has the foundations, whose builder and architect is God." In other words, in the God of glory he saw the city of God. Do you get it? In the God of glory, he saw the city of God. He did not see the city of God as a thing. He saw the city of God as somehow, something to do with the person of God, with the being of God, with the life of God, with the salvation of God, with the calling of God. Do you see it like that?

When you come to the end of the Book, in Revelation 21 and 22, you read that this city at the end of the Book is an extraordinary city. I believe I am right in saying this: it is 1500 miles high[1], 1500 miles wide, and 1500 miles deep. Now I find that extraordinary! For it to be 1500 miles deep and 1500 miles wide, okay, but 1500 miles up? That is something! Then it has twelve gates. Alright, we have no problem there. I mean there is what I think could be almost 1500 miles going above one of the gates, I suppose, but it has only one street. Now, that is a problem; that is a real problem, isn't it? We talk about all these golden streets, yet it says there is only one street. It only speaks of *a street* in the singular. So, someone says, "Well, that's alright … it's a spiral." I know that one day in one of these sort-of science-fiction things they come up with, cities are going to be suspended in the air, and all the rest of it.

You know, really and truthfully, I do not think that city is meant to be understood literally. Now, don't get me wrong, I do believe that there will be a literal city because there is a new heaven and a new earth and we are going to have bodies that can eat. We know this because our Lord Jesus has a redemption

---

1 See Revelation 21:16 "And the city lieth foursquare, and the length thereof is as great as the breadth: and he measured the city with the reed, twelve thousand furlongs: the length and the breadth and the height thereof are equal." 12,000 furlongs is equal to 1500 miles.

body and He ate broiled fish and bread. You will remember that. So, we know that we are going to have actual bodies which are located. We shall be able to go through walls. Think of that: just straight through the wall! That will be lovely. We will be able to go through closed doors and that kind of thing. We will have bodies that are located and therefore there will be some kind of city, I am sure. There will be some kind of location. I am quite sure about that.

When we come to the city at the end of the Book, it is quite clear to me that this city is a spiritual reality. God is using simple language to express a reality. Why? I will tell you why, because I have never, in my little life, ever heard a husband refer to his wife as his city. Have you? I mean, she may look like fortified bulwarks and towers and turrets, but I have never heard a husband say, "My beloved city is over there." Or, "May I introduce to you the municipality?" You have never heard anyone referred to like that—no, of course not.

Zion as the Bride of Christ

The Bible speaks of the bride of Christ, the wife of the Lamb, as the *city* of God. That is because you have two things. On the one side you have a bride. What does a bride symbolise? The most intimate union known to mankind. Two people becoming one. It is the most intimate relationship possible. Now that is the one side of Zion. God longs for a union which is intimate, an eternal union with Himself. It is not a matter of technique. It is not a matter of doctrine. It is not just a matter of method. It is not just a question of the science of government. It is a question of love—

first love—right the way through. It is an eternal relationship of love. How wonderful!

Did you realise your Lord loves you so much that He wants to bring you into this? That He wants to bring me into this? He wants to bring all of us into such a relationship with Himself. If we should love Him like that because He loves us, how much should we love one another? The whole thing is a love relationship. (We will come to that later when we look at Isaiah 58.) However, you see the real point I am trying to get at just now is the very simple thing that when the Lord speaks about the bride, His wife, He is speaking of a very intimate thing, a union with Himself which is eternal and is so intimate.

Zion as the Centre of Government

But when you speak of a city, you speak of a metropolis. You speak of a centre of government, a centre of administration. That is the other side of Zion. That is ruling. You know there is going to be a new heaven and a new earth, but God needs people who are going to rule it. Are you going to leave that just to one or two old ones?

Dear friends, I want to tell you something. Just because we are here in this company does not mean that we are all going to rule. Some of us are incapable of ruling a tiny little portion of our household, let alone ruling in the kingdom. Unless God can teach you and me how to get the victory down here and how to reign with Christ down here, we cannot reign there.

Zion, a Glorious City

You see, what I am really trying to say is that what the Lord means by Zion is really something glorious. No wonder the psalmist says, "Glorious things are spoken of thee, O city of God" (Psalm 87:3) … "The Lord loveth the gates of Zion" (Psalm 87:2). Now, if that does not inflame you with some kind of desire for knowing the Lord in a deeper way, and in understanding this whole matter of what His heart's purpose is, I don't know what will.

That Zion is produced out of certain materials—precious stones, pearl, and gold. Where are they produced? They are produced here, down here, not up in the 'never-never.' They are produced down here in our relationships with one another, in our relationships at work, in all the problems and experiences and vicissitudes of life. That is where the gold of His nature, the precious stone of His life, and the pearl of His suffering is wrought in us. That is the material out of which that city is being built. The bride is being produced out of that—Christ in you, the hope of glory.

Do you not want more of Him? How can we get more of Him? Well, this is just where we can get into deception. Sometimes people tell me they can get more of Him by just going away and being alone. Now, I am quite sure there are real dangers in fellowship when we rest so much on one another that we do not have any life of our own with the Lord. That is a terrible danger! But so is the other danger when people think that they can go off and be on their own and grow in the Lord. My dear friend, it is a form of escapism. It can be a form of deception. You can go off, shut yourself off from all the problems of your brothers and sisters and seemingly grow and grow and grow. You are not growing at all. It is in the rough house of the church down here that we really grow—in our relationships with one another, in the way we go through, in the way we open up to one another, in the way we are built together, and in the way we really share the life of the Lord together. That is where it happens.

So you see, coming back to this wonderful chapter in Isaiah. Did you hear what the Lord said? Listen again to those words in Isaiah 61:1–3: "The Spirit of the Lord God is upon Me; [This is of Jesus the Messiah.] because the Lord hath anointed Me to preach good tidings unto the meek; He hath sent me to bind up the broken-hearted, to proclaim liberty to the captives, and opening of the prisons to them that are bound; to proclaim the year of the Lord's favour, and the day of the vengeance of our God to comfort all that mourn; to appoint unto them that mourn in Zion, to give unto them a garland for ashes, the oil of joy for mourning, the garment of praise for the spirit of heaviness; that they may be called trees of righteousness, [That is something living.] the planting of the Lord, [That is something that originates with God.] that He may be glorified." It ends in glory.

Then comes this—listen: "And they shall build the old wastes, they shall raise up the former desolations, and they shall repair the waste cities, the desolations of many generations. Strangers shall stand and feed your flocks and foreigners shall be your plowmen and your vinedressers. But ye shall be called, the priests of the Lord; men shall call you the ministers of our God" (verses 4–6a).

In other words, it begins with the ministry of our Lord and ends with the building of Zion. It begins with the loosing of the bonds. It begins with the bringing out of the dungeon, out of the prison. It begins with the garment of praise for the spirit of heaviness, with joy for mourning. It begins with all these wonderful things and it ends with the building of all that has laid waste for generations. Whether it is the first building of Zion, or whether it is the restoration of Zion, or whether it is the completion of Zion, it does not matter. Who is the builder? The Lord Jesus is the builder. He said, "Upon this rock I will build My church and the gates of Hell shall not prevail against it" (Matthew 16:18). That is why we have those wonderful words, "For Zion's sake I will not hold my peace, and for Jerusalem's sake I will not rest, until her righteousness go forth as brightness, and her salvation as a lamp that burneth" (Isaiah 62:1). The Lord Jesus intercedes at this very moment for this whole matter of the building up of Zion. Well, I hope that you just understand a little of that. He has a determination. He is the builder of Zion and I want to know where you stand.

"The Set Time"

It says in Psalm 102, "The set time has come." This is a beautiful Psalm, a beautiful little word. Psalm 102:12–16, "But thou, O Lord, wilt abide for ever; and thy memorial name unto all generations. Thou wilt arise, and have mercy upon Zion; for it is time to have pity upon her, yea, the set time is come. For thy servants take pleasure in her stones, and have pity upon her dust. So the nations shall fear the name of the Lord, and all the kings of the earth thy glory. For the Lord hath built up Zion; He hath appeared in his glory." Did you hear that? The set time has come. What a wonderful thing it is when the set time has come for the building up of Zion!

You know in church history there have been some glorious appointments. Pentecost was one. There have been some glorious appointments since then. We can just mention a few of them. The Reformation was certainly one of them and the Wesleyan era was certainly another. The Brethren era was certainly another and so has been the outpouring of the Spirit in our own day; that is another. It has been a set time. What is the Lord's object in it? Is it just to make the saints happy? Not just that. He wants us to be happy, but His real objective is to build up Zion. There is something eternal.

You know, you have one short life if you live your full span of 70 years. Many here will not live that; others will live longer. However, we have only one set span of life and in that one short span of years either God builds you into Zion, or not. One day when you look back, your whole experience here will be like a pinhead—your birth, your life, your salvation, all your experiences will all seem just like a little tiny pinhead compared with an endless eternity. You will marvel at the grace of God, that in that one little pinhead of time, He did something. Then, oh, that God would deliver us from regrets! That in that little pinhead of time I refused to let the Lord do this and that in my life, and I wouldn't let Him have His way there, and I wouldn't settle this issue, and I wouldn't allow Him to lead me into this or that. Dear friends, we shall regret it for the whole of eternity, won't we? I would. Wouldn't you? To see that you held on to some stupid little issue in your life that you thought would please you and lost an eternity of usefulness to God. You won't lose your salvation, but you could lose an eternity of usefulness to God. Think of the joy of having a position in the government of God. Think of the joy of having a position in the Zion of God, of having a position as being part of the bride of Christ, the wife of the

Lamb, how wonderful! When it is seen like that you understand why Paul spoke of our light affliction which is but for a moment and worketh for us an exceeding and eternal weight of glory. Of course you see it when you understand it like that; you can see it in no other way. Isn't it true?

Listen to what this Psalmist says. If he says the set time is come, he says, "Thy servants take pleasure in her stones and have pity upon her dust." I don't know whether you have any pleasure in the living stones around you. I think some of us, all we ever see are all the sort-of faults, blemishes, breakdowns, failures, and everything else about the living stones around us. However, it says, "Thy servants take pleasure in her stones." What a wonderful thing it would be if I could see you as one of those stones that God has quarried out of the life of Christ and take pleasure in it! If you could see me as a living stone quarried out of the life of Christ and take pleasure in it. "Have pity upon her dust." I don't think we have too much pity upon her dust frankly. We do not show, always, very much pity to one another when it comes to these things.

Well, I think that is enough for now, but isn't it marvellous that God has made a divine provision of grace and power for the building of Zion. We have talked all about Zion and if you are born of God you are in Zion, you are born of Zion, you're registered in Zion, you have got the highways to Zion (or should have) in your heart. What about starting to walk in them? It does not matter how young you are, you can take the first step right now. You can go to the Lord on your own and say, "Lord, I want to walk worthily of the calling with which You have called me. I want to begin to understand this matter."

It won't be all that long before all that we see is shaken and disappears. We speak about being in the last part of the age, but none of us really finally face up to what it is going to mean to live in the last days. As I said before, I am not the least bit afraid about it. It's wonderful! Yet we need to face up to the fact that you are not going to have months and months, certainly not years' warning (and I very much doubt that you are going to have months' warning), in which you can suddenly turn around, turn over a new leaf, start to learn all the lessons you ought to have learned over the years, and really get the experience you should have had—you cannot do it. What you need to do, if you are wise in the Lord, is start now. Very simply. You start with the King, not with the kingdom. Start with the King. Really have it out with the Lord and start with Him. Then, when you have got your relationship right with Him, begin to get your relationship right with others. Then, God will start to do this work of building up Zion amongst us and then maybe, praise God, we shall know something of the glory of God appearing in Zion and His ruling out of Zion. May He do it.

Shall we pray?

Lord, we have talked about Zion and Lord it can either be just a subject that is sort of a dusty subject, a biblical subject or, Lord, Thou canst make it a living reality to us. Thou couldst take just one thing, oh Lord, and shine it like a shaft of light into our hearts. Lord, wilt Thou do that? Grant Lord, that that spirit of wisdom and revelation will be given to us in this matter. Bring this home to us, Lord.

We pray that those who are really young in Thee, those who are just in the early years of their life would know Thee as Lord and Saviour. Lord, won't Thou reveal this matter of Zion to such? We pray it may come to those who are older with real freshness, Lord, like a clarification from on high. For those who are young, let it come with all that glorious illuminating power of the Holy Spirit. Lord, we pray that we shall all be found really seeking for the city which has the foundations whose builder and maker is Thyself and Lord, we ask this together in the name of our Lord Jesus. Amen.

3.
Travail for Zion

Isaiah 62

For Zion's sake will I not hold my peace, and for Jerusalem's sake I will not rest, until her righteousness go forth as brightness, and her salvation as a lamp that burneth. And the nations shall see thy righteousness, and all kings thy glory, and thou shalt be called by a new name, which the mouth of the Lord shall name. Thou shalt also be a crown of beauty in the hand of the Lord, and a royal diadem in the hand of thy God. Thou shalt no more be termed

Forsaken; neither shall thy land any more be termed Desolate: but thou shalt be called Hephzi-bah, and thy land Beulah; for the Lord delighteth in thee, and thy land shall be married. For as a young man marrieth a virgin, so shall thy sons marry thee; and as the bridegroom rejoiceth over the bride, so shall thy God rejoice over thee.

I have set watchmen upon thy walls, O Jerusalem; they shall never hold their peace day nor night: ye that are the Lord's remembrancers, take ye no rest, and give him no rest, till he establish, and till he make Jerusalem a praise in the earth. The Lord hath sworn by his right hand, and by the arm of his strength, Surely I will no more give thy grain to be food for thine enemies; and foreigners shall not drink thy new wine, for which thou hast labored: but they that have garnered it shall eat it, and praise the Lord; and they that have gathered it shall drink it in the courts of my sanctuary.

Go through, go through the gates; prepare ye the way of the people; cast up, cast up the highway; gather out the stones; lift up an ensign for the peoples. Behold, the Lord hath proclaimed unto the end of the earth, Say ye to the daughter of Zion, Behold, thy salvation cometh; behold, his reward is with him, and his recompense before him. And they shall call them The holy people, The redeemed of the Lord: and thou shalt be called Sought out, a city not forsaken.

I want to talk now about the travail of Zion. We have spent time on the battle over Zion as well as the building of Zion. This time I want to talk a little while about the travail for Zion. We find it in this 62nd chapter of Isaiah: "For Zion's sake will I not hold my peace, and for Jerusalem's sake I will not rest, until her righteousness go forth as brightness, and her salvation as a lamp that burneth." Verse six: "I have set My watchmen upon thy walls, O Jerusalem; they shall never hold their peace day nor night: ye that are the Lord's remembrancers, take ye no rest, and give Him no rest, till He establish, and till He make Jerusalem a praise in the earth."

Shall we just bow together in a word of prayer? Let us all look to the Lord once more in a definite way that He would come to us.

Father, we thank Thee that Thou hast given us an anointing in our Lord Jesus. It is the person of the Holy Spirit who makes that anointing a glorious reality. We thank Thee that for speaker or for hearer there is that anointing provided. Lord, now we just want to simply confess before Thee that we can do nothing without Thee, but Lord, with Thee, in Thee, and through Thee we can do all things. So beloved Lord, we thank Thee, Thy word can come to us in living power and will and we can hear it in living power and we will. Dear Lord, we praise Thee for Thy gracious provision. Make Thy Word live to us, Lord, we pray. We ask it in the name of our Lord Jesus. Amen.

Now, who is speaking in this chapter 62 of Isaiah? It is, in one sense, a little problem for us. Is it the Lord who speaks through the mouth of the prophet in Isaiah 61:1? I think all of you know, of course, that we were not given these scriptures in chapters and verses. Someone at a much later date reduced all these scriptures to chapter and verse. We must be very thankful for it because these chapters and verses are a great help, not only in memorisation but in quick and easy reference. How could we possibly put our finger on something in Psalm 119 if we did not have verses? Think of it! Or Jeremiah, with his enormous number of chapters. I mean, if there were no chapters and no verses, think what problem we would have trying to find something and being able to refer somebody else to it. We would have a terrible job. But someone reduced it to chapters and verses.

However, some folks have got this idea that the Lord sort of dictated it, you know, by saying, "This is chapter 62 coming up, verse one ... and then verse two now ... and verse three following." Of course, it did not come like that at all. We have now these scriptures, we have their chapters, we have the verses for our help, but now and again, very unfortunately, it tends to hold back our understanding of the Word. In other words, it sometimes breaks up the continuity of a passage.

Now in chapter 61, verse one, we have the Lord Jesus, the Messiah, speaking: "The Spirit of the Lord God is upon Me; because the Lord hath anointed Me to preach good tidings [of the gospel] unto the meek;" and so on. However, in verse ten we have the prophet speaking: "I will greatly rejoice in the Lord, my soul shall be joyful in my God; for He hath clothed me with the garments of salvation, He hath covered me with the robe of righteousness, as a bridegroom decketh himself with a garland, and a bride adorneth herself with her jewels."

So, we then have a problem when we come to chapter 62, verse one. Is it the prophet Isaiah who says, "For Zion's sake, will I not hold my peace, and for Jerusalem's sake I will not rest, until her righteousness go forth as brightness, and her salvation as a lamp that burneth," or is it the Messiah? It makes no difference for us, in one sense, insofar as whether it is the prophet Isaiah who is speaking or the Messiah; it is travail. It is divinely given travail. It is travail that has been conceived by the Holy Spirit.

It is my conviction that the one who speaks at the beginning of Isaiah 62 is not the prophet, but it is the Messiah. We have therefore, as it were, a tremendously instructive revelation of the burden which is on the heart of the Messiah. We have a window into His intercessory ministry. We know He ever lives to make intercession for us. He has appeared before the Father's face for us and here we have, as it were, a little window into that unceasing ministry at the right hand of God.

Now having said that, let us take a look at this chapter. It falls very easily for us into three parts. First of all, in the first five verses we have the determination of the Lord revealed. Then, in verses six to nine we have the fellowship of the Lord introduced. After that, in verses ten to twelve we have the challenge of the Lord to us.

The Determination of the Lord

First of all is the determination of the Lord. "For Zion's sake," He says, "I will not hold my peace, and for Jerusalem's sake I will not rest, until her righteousness go forth as brightness, and her salvation as a lamp that burneth." At the very heart of His travail is Zion and Jerusalem. In other words, this whole matter we have been talking about is the key to the whole purpose of God. It is why we have been saved. It is why He has brought us into union with Himself and why He has anointed us with the Holy Spirit. This is why, indeed, there is a creation at all, why there is a universe. It is why there may be other universes beyond that. It is why He created man and why He created man in His image. This is why, in some inexplicable mystery, He allowed man to fall and why He sent forth a redeemer, the Lord Jesus. Zion, Jerusalem—it is on the heart of the Lord Jesus. If Zion is on His heart, I want it to be on mine.

Spiritual things are so simple. Of course, sometimes when we first hear a new truth, it seems to us to be so hard to take in. We think, "Oh, how deep it is! How complex it is!" but, in actual fact, when we *see* something, it is utter simplicity. All the really essential truths are utter simplicity—profound—but utter simplicity. Really, if my life is a mess because I do not know whether I should go this way or go that way, I do not know if I should take this step or that step, I get worried about this and I get worried about that, how simple it is at least to get hold of this one thing: whatever is on His heart must be of vital importance to me. If my life can, in some simple way, become centred upon that matter which is central to our Lord's burden and concern, then surely a whole lot of things are going to fall into place. Business, family life, personal problems, background problems, national problems, international things, they are all going to somehow fall into place when once we see what it is that is on His heart and what it means.

It is one thing just to have Zion as a name, as we have said, but that does not mean anything if we only understand it as some strange idea. The point is to see what Zion really means, what it is that the Lord has called *Zion*, what He means by that "Jerusalem which is above." We have it put very beautifully here: "For Zion's sake will I not hold my peace, and for Jerusalem's sake I will not rest, until her righteousness go forth as a lamp." This little word here, "For Zion's sake will I not hold my peace," is interesting. In the Hebrew, there is a little word that means *to be silent*, as it is in the New American Standard Bible, "I will not keep silent." Well, this first word in Hebrew just means *to be silent, to be inactive,* or *to be still*. Our Lord says, "For Zion's sake I will not be silent, I will not be still, I will not be inactive." That is perfect.

The second word is a word we use in Hebrew. Anyone who has been to Israel must surely have heard some father or mother or someone else—especially if you live in the place where I live—bawl out from the window, "Sheket!" It just means, "Shut up," or "Silence! Be quiet!" This is the word exactly. The Lord says, "I will not be quiet; I will not be undisturbed." Well, now that is interesting, isn't it? If this really is a revelation of the heart of the Lord, that He says, "I will not be inactive, I will not be still, I will not be silent, I will not be quiet or undisturbed. There is something that disturbs Me. There is something that, as it were, gives me cause for real concern."

There is another lovely thing here. This was Zion, of course, or Jerusalem. Then He says about this Jerusalem, in the asv, "until her righteousness go forth as brightness, and her salvation as a lamp that burneth." Here is something I find very, very beautiful. First of all, this word *brightness* is a very unusual word. In Hebrew it is a girl's name, *Nogah*. It just means the kind of clear sunshine, particularly the clear clarity, after rain. So, after a tempest, after the storm, it is that wonderful clear vision when you can see miles and miles and miles.

If you want to see where it is used, it is used in II Samuel 23:4 in a very beautiful and well-known passage when King David was dying: "A morning without clouds, when the tender grass springeth out of the earth, through clear shining after rain." Clear shining after rain. Now isn't that a lovely thought? The Lord says, "I will not be quiet, I will not be inactive, I will not be undisturbed, until for Zion's sake, for Jerusalem's sake, until her righteousness go forth as clear sunshine after the tempest. Clear as crystal."

Then we have this other beautiful word, "... and her salvation as a lamp that burneth." For those of us who are Bible students, it would be very interesting if the word here in the Hebrew for lamp was the *menorah*, you know, the seven-branched lamp. Then we would be able to take it up with Zechariah 4 and go on to Revelation 1 and so on. It would be most interesting, but it is not the word for menorah. It is the word for a torch—a burning torch, a flaming torch—but here is something beautiful. We have got Jesus in this. For the very word that is used for salvation is the word that literally has His name in the heart of it: Yeshua[1], in Hebrew. "Until *Jesus* go forth as a lamp that burneth." The knowledge of Jesus. The salvation of Jesus. Isn't it wonderful when you think of it like that? There it is right there, His whole name right in this word. Of course, it means *salvation*. So, I found this rather wonderful, this whole determination of the Lord.

The Lord's Desire

What is the Lord's desire? His desire is that Zion and Jerusalem shall be like a flaming torch giving light everywhere, in the light of which nations may come to know God. In this light, peoples may find the Lord, they may come into an experience of the salvation of the Lord; that is the longing of the Lord. Insofar as you and I are part of that spiritual Zion, we are meant to be that right where we are. Wherever there is a company of the Lord's people really gathered together on the foundation of the Lord Jesus and in His name, they are meant to be like a flaming torch in the light of

1 Strongs #3444

which the people of the community may find God, may know God, may see God, may experience God; the salvation of the Lord may burn like a lamp, shine like a lamp with brightness and clarity. Oh, we live in a world of confusion, of perplexity, but we have this concern of the Lord that somehow or other His Zion, His Jerusalem shall be clear shining. Righteousness is clear shining.

Now, we have no righteousness of our own, have we? We know that. The more we go on with the Lord, the more we know this one simple fact, that we have no righteousness of our own. It is His righteousness, but oh, if the nations would only see His righteousness. If they could only see His justifying grace and power in and through us, wouldn't it be wonderful? I fear that sometimes all they see is storm. All they see is tempest. All they see is smoke. The fire has long since gone out. They just see something that is like a damp squib amongst the people of God—no dynamic, no fire, no power, and no light.

However, the Lord's determination has never changed. At the very beginning He said. "Upon this rock I will build My church and the gates of hell shall not prevail against it" (Matthew 16:18). He has never at any single point given up His responsibilities for the building of the church. Thank God for that! Nor did He say He will build the church until the antichrist comes, or until the middle of the twentieth century, when things will become so complex and difficult and all the rest of it, that He will give it all over to the enemy, as some appear to believe. No. He said He will build His church right through to the end. We have that wonderful word in Zechariah, "and the top stone shall be brought forth with shouts of, 'Grace, grace, unto it,'" (Zechariah 4:7) right in the very midst of all the storm, and all the battle, and all the foment of evil of the powers of darkness. Right in the midst of it all, the work will be completed by the grace of God. The grace of God began it, the grace of God developed it, the grace of God watched over every single movement of the Head, of the Spirit, in the history of its construction, and the grace of God will complete it.

Dear ones, what a wonderful joy it is that we are in that period when we may well see with our own eyes, the completion of the work! Isn't that marvellous? It is so wonderful, either to be on the beginning of something, or the end of something. I always feel sorry for the people who are in the middle of it, because that is the real routine just going on, plodding on and on and on. We may have storms and troubles, we may have much that is going to come upon the face of the earth, but we also have some glorious privileges which no other generation of the saints had within the last part of the age. Therefore, we are going to see the completion of the house of God, by the grace of God! Now if it said, "by the power of God, or by the devotion of His people, or by the zeal of the Lord's people," I should be very worried indeed. But since it says the last thing they will gasp is, "Grace, grace unto it," I have every confidence that this thing is going to be done.

So, why should we give up? Why should we fear? Why should we become discouraged? Why should we become worn out by the enemy's devices and weapons? If this is what His desire is for the church, that her righteousness burn as a brightness, and her salvation as a lamp that burneth, we have got a tremendous comfort. I feel that if our Lord is praying like that, there is every chance it is going to get answered. I would rather be on His side than anybody else's, thank you. If there are those who feel that somehow or other, the whole thing is going to be snuffed out, it is all going to go into darkness, and all the rest of it, okay, let them, if they want to believe that. But as far as I am concerned, if our Lord is still going to pray that right through to the very end, then I want to side with Him. I want to be with Him and I want to be involved in this matter. So, we have His determination.

Now, the full answer to this burden of the Messiah will only be realised when He returns, so let us make that quite clear. It is only when He actually finally returns with glory and great power, that this Zion will then be a lamp that burns to the ends of the earth, for the Word of God says the nations will walk in the light of it—this city, this Zion. It says expressly in Revelation 21:23–24 that the nations will walk in the light of it. It says it has no need of the light of sun or moon, for the glory of God will lighten it and the Lamb will be the lamp thereof, and the nations shall walk in the light of it. Well, praise the Lord. When He does come, then this is going to be finally realised.

What about the travail that is required for that purpose of the Lord to be fulfilled? It is not just going to come automatically. We cannot just face it in a fatalistic manner and say, "Well, it's the will of God. He is going to do it. He is all powerful. It will be all right."

The fact of the matter is that this full answer to our Lord's great burden here, is going to be then and that is why He goes on to say, "… and thou shalt be called by a new name, which the mouth of the Lord shall name," or designate. Then He says, "Thou shalt be a crown of beauty in the hand of the Lord, a royal diadem in the hand of thy God." What wonderful words!

First, you shall be called "… by a new name." We know in the first chapters of Revelation that our Lord says to the overcomers, to those who finally become part of that eternal Zion, He says to them, "and My Father will give you a new name, which no one knows but he who receives it." It is wonderful.

Then, "a crown of beauty." Now, this may take away a little bit of it for you, because you are all used to those wonderful crowns at the Tower of London. I remember when I went there years ago. (I had forgotten all about the Tower. I had a macabre interest in the Bloody Tower where they had all those bodies sort of all stacked in serried ranks [rows standing together], under that little green lawn somewhere.) However, I must say that what absolutely caught me were the crown jewels. I had never seen anything like it! I stood there gawking for quite some while just looking at those jewels. What a crown! Then, of course, I thought to myself, "How does the Queen ever wear that great heavy thing on her head?" Incredible!

Now, it may disappoint you, but the first crown here is really a wreath. In the old days, that was the kind of crowns they had, but it was still a wreath, or a garland of beauty, or glory as is the word in Hebrew. It is an unusual word. It is not the usual word for glory. It does mean beauty, but it is somewhere in between— glorious beauty. A wreath of glorious beauty is perhaps the best way we could put it.

Then the other lovely word, "a royal diadem." This is a turban. I am sure some might be quite upset by that, but in the old days, the potentates of the East wore a royal turban. It was still a symbol of absolute authority. Only the king could wear that turban. It was a royal turban. Somehow I love the word diadem, because for us in the West I suppose it has a real feeling of power. Don't you think it has? As soon I hear the word diadem I think of authority, regal authority, absolute authority. Of course, those of you from the States, I suppose don't quite appreciate this, but when we in Britain think of a diadem we think of something with absolute authority. Well, don't be put off by the thought that it is a turban because it means just the same—absolute authority.

Our Lord has said this and so we know it is going to be so in those days. We are told of the beauty and the glory that is going to be revealed through that Zion of God, through the Bride, the wife of the Lamb, when the Lord and His Bride are finally brought together and God's glory fills them and it is manifested through them. It is going to be absolutely marvellous. The authority—It is going to be a city with great authority. A new name, glory, and dominion! Isn't the whole of it wonderful?

We do not want just to put it all in the future, because you see, there have been many, many times in the history of God's people when the Lord by the Holy Spirit has come in like a great tide. When that has happened, Zion's righteousness has gone forth as brightness, and her salvation as a lamp that burneth. I think of the Reformation period. Oh, how glorious a thing it was when the Lord overturned the whole institutional thing and for at least a generation the salvation of Zion went forth as a lamp that burneth! It was like a flaming torch held up. It was not just a question of personalities (there were great personalities in it, one after another), but dear friends, it was as if the people of God caught fire by the Holy Spirit and the whole of it went to the ends of the earth! It turned Europe upside down.

It was the same with the Moravians. It was the same with the Quakers—that despised people—but my word, what happened when the Holy Spirit got hold of George Fox and a few others and turned the whole of Britain upside down! Why, did you know that sometimes more than two-thirds of the travelling preachers were in prison at one time? Think of that. I do not suppose many denominations ever had two-thirds of its ministers in prison. What did they do? They turned the prisons upside down. Many of them died in those prisons, but out of those prisons came convicts who became flaming evangelists and prophets, saved by the testimony of men who died in chains! It was a salvation that was like a flaming torch held up so that the whole country heard. As a result, our prisons were reformed. Quaker ladies went and sat in rat-infested, vile and wicked places, and by their very purity of life and testimony, simply transformed the places from inside.

Not only those, think of the Wesleyans, that great movement of the Spirit when it first began. My, it was a lamp! It was a salvation, burning like a lamp, wasn't it? It is tremendous what happened in this country, in these islands, and in the United States as well, through George Whitfield, John Wesley, and those other great men of God in that move of the Spirit.

Now, these are just a few examples. We could go back earlier to other periods before the Reformation. We could mention many others since then, but what a wonderful time it has been every time the Holy Spirit has come in and this travail of the Lord and of others has been answered and realised, if only in part. Suddenly, the righteousness of Zion and Jerusalem, God's spiritual Zion, has gone forth as brightness like clear shining after tempest and storm. Her salvation has gone to the ends of the earth like a flaming torch.

Don't you think that you and I need something of this? We want to see it in our day, don't we? Oh, that God would do it in Britain, that God would do it in the nations of Europe, that God would do it in the whole Free World. Thank God He is doing it in very large parts of the world behind the Iron Curtain and the Bamboo Curtain—salvation as a lamp that burneth. My, how wonderful it is when we hear on the BBC that it is conservatively estimated that 60 million of the citizens of the Soviet Union are believers in the Almighty. Isn't it incredible? To keep the youngsters out of the churches, they have had to show what they normally call the depraved films of the West, on Easter Sunday and Good Friday. For the last two years in Russia, they have had nonstop showings of what they normally call depraved. (Now, we would not call them depraved, I mean, Mickey Mouse and that kind of thing, but the Soviets have called these depraved for years.) It is interesting, isn't it, that a tiny little clique at the top can hold a whole nation in absolute bondage? What clear evidence it is that it is God who is behind it all. Normally speaking, you would not think that so many millions of people could be held in such bondage, but when God's time comes for that bondage to be broken, it will be broken.

What about us in the Free World? Abortion, bloodguiltiness, pornography, evil on every side, our whole school system being infiltrated by ideas that have not been tested, and which in the end may lead to tragedy in many young lives, what are we to do? What we need is that kind of move of the Holy Spirit, that will mean that the salvation of Zion will go forth and will burn as a torch! Her righteousness will go forth as brightness. Well, I find all that, very, very exciting.

There is another lovely little thing here in this chapter. It says, "Thou shalt no more be termed Forsaken; neither shall thy land any more be termed Desolate" (Isaiah 62:4). Think of these words forsaken and desolate. Have you ever seen something forsaken? It is empty and derelict, isn't it? It has got a feeling of past glory. If you have ever been somewhere, to a place, a house, or something that in times past has been glorious, and now it is forsaken, it has that awful atmosphere of dereliction. A land that is desolate.

You know, so much of the Lord's work comes into that category. It has an atmosphere of dereliction about it. We have the meetings, we have the activities, we have the preaching, we have all the round of things, but somehow or other, it is forsaken. Somehow it has become divorced from its owner. Then the Lord says about this, "Thou shalt no more be termed Forsaken; neither shall thy land any more be termed Desolate: but thou shalt be called Hephzibah." As you probably know, Hephzibah is a lady's name. Now, the interesting thing is that this just means, "My delight is in her." So, the Lord says, "Not forsaken, My delight is in her." He has not departed, but His delight is in her. That is much more than "I love her," more than, "I have an affection for her, she is very interesting." He says, "My delight is in her." That is emotive language, isn't it? My delight is in her—His heart is in this, captured by her.

Then of course, He calls her Beulah, *married*. In Hebrew, everything comes from roots. You have a root word and all these other meanings become very, very thrilling. The language is exciting, just simply for that reason. Forgive me any women's libbers here, but unfortunately Hebrew is a language that does not take into consideration anything to do with women's liberation at all. It may shock you to know that the word *baal*, which we think of as such a bad word, is in fact the word *ba'al*, the word for husband, Lord. The word marriage comes from *ba'al bet olah*. Do you see? It really just means *Lorded* or *owned*. Well, of course I know, women's liberation does not like this kind of thing anymore, but that is what the Bible says. The Lord says you shall no more be called desolate, but you shall be called *owned, married*, brought into union, brought into possession. Well, that's wonderful!

Then He goes on and says something to you fathers and mothers here, and to any of you who are concerned about the new generation. I think it is tremendous because He does not say what you would think if you will look at it: "For as a young man marrieth a virgin, so shall thy sons marry thee" (see verse 5). What is the great tragedy of Christian work? It is that the children do not grow up in the faith of their parents. Somewhere along the line they see hypocrisy, or they see something which does not work, or they see something that is not real and so they turn away from it. It is the cry all over the world. Don't feel condemned. There are great servants of the Lord whose children are black sheep, as black as it is possible to be.

I have often had much to do with different servants of the Lord and I have heard those dear white-haired fathers, now grandfathers, groaning over the ways they dealt with their children in earlier days. Yet, the promise of the Lord is: "thy sons shall marry thee." Now if it said, "For the Lord will marry you," I would understand, but the Lord actually says, the new generation of Zion, shall be wedded to the old. The new generation will come into a union with the old. They will marry you; your sons will marry you.

He goes on and says, "And as the bridegroom rejoiceth over the bride so shall thy God rejoice over thee" (see verse 5). What a wonderfully gracious intimation of the Lord's purpose! You know, this whole question of Zion's salvation, burning as a lamp to the ends of the earth, her righteousness going forth as brightness, is also a matter of the new generation. There must be a people who are prepared to travail for the new generation. It is not a question of just teaching them. It is not just a question of imposing ideas upon them. The real need is for people who will get behind the scenes and understand the burden on the heart of the Lord, and really travail for them, so that there will be another generation, not a second generation, in one sense, but a second generation in the spirit of the verse. Wedded!

There is one thing that is forbidden in Scripture, and that is for sons to marry their mother, but the Lord speaks of your sons marrying you. What can He mean, since it is a forbidden relationship? What can he mean? He means simply this: that that new generation will come into such a union with the past generation, that they will live in a contemporary way, and speak in a contemporary way, and dress in a contemporary way, and yet have the same faith, the same experience, the same power, and the same knowledge and experience of that salvation of the Lord. They will also be in Zion. If you are a father or a mother, isn't it a tremendous comfort to you that our Lord has actually said something about a new generation, your sons? He said it. It is all part of this matter. We have many growing up amongst us and we have a burden for them.

The Fellowship of the Lord

What about the fellowship of the Lord in this matter? We have it in Isaiah 62:6–9: "I have set watchmen upon thy walls, O Jerusalem; they shall never hold their peace, day nor night." "*Watchmen* set on thy walls," isn't this a very interesting word? This word for watchmen can also be *god*. Indeed, today in modern Hebrew, we speak of the police in the same way; we speak of them as *watchmen* or *gods*. It is the same word in Hebrew. Of course, our Lord is not saying "I have set policemen, on thy walls, O Jerusalem" because immediately we would get the idea of someone telling everybody else what to do, or what they should not do. However, *watchmen* is the best way of saying it, although it has the thought of *god*.

What does a watchman do? He watches what is going on outside the walls of the city, and he also watches what is happening on the inside. He guards the city; he watches the city. If, in a single moment of time there is a problem, then immediately he will send an alert about any problem coming from a distance. He will immediately see it. The farther off he sees it, the better for the whole city. The sooner he spots the problem or danger coming, the better it is for the whole. The Lord has set watchmen on the walls of this Zion of His. This Zion that He has so much concern for, that He loves so greatly, that He has this determination over, He has watchmen on the walls watching and guarding.

Then will you notice that these watchmen do something which is very interesting? He says, "They shall never hold their peace day nor night." Now, here is one great excuse for never shutting up. The Lord says about these watchmen: they will never shut up.

They will never hold their peace. He uses exactly the same word of Himself. He said, "I will not hold my peace." He will not be silent, He will not be inactive, He will not be still. It is rather wonderful when you think of it like that, isn't? Somehow or other, here is the fellowship of the Lord. He says He will not be still; He will not be inactive. Now He says, I have watchmen on the walls that will not be inactive. They have come into My activity. They have come into My refusal to be silent, or to be quiet, or to be still. They have got the same Spirit in them.

What does it mean that these watchmen are on the walls in Zion? They are not just in Zion. Will you note this? They are on the walls. What does it mean? Please think. You have often heard this verse quoted, either in prayer, or in preaching, but what does it mean *watchmen on the walls*? It means this: these are people who are totally committed to the purpose of God. They are not only *in* Zion, they are *on the walls* of Zion. They do not merely travail for others to be in the will of God; they are sure that they are themselves in the will of God first.

Here is a little point: it is very possible to be deceived in this whole matter of prayer and to get a kind of prayer complex, where we just simply pray and pray. We mouth things and mouth petitions. We go on and on and on, and actually become alienated from the mind of God because our prayer can become an activity (you understand what I mean), rather than something coming out of union with the Lord. We have a capacity by which we can do it. We can do it with Bible study, with prayer, with our meetings, with church life, and with everything. We can turn it into a *thing* instead of it coming out of union with the Lord, out of, as it were, sensitivity to Himself.

Do you understand what I am trying to say on this matter? Perhaps some of you do not, but if you will pray about it, I am sure the Lord will help you with this. It is no good saying, as I have heard people say, "Oh, I must pray that the church of God be recovered," yet they are not in any recovery themselves. They say, "Oh, I must pray that the Lord will do this and do that," while they are not themselves committed. It is as if somehow or other they can pray for it and in their own lives have a complete contradiction to it. Do you understand what I am saying? In other words, if you are going to pray for Zion, you must be committed to Zion. If you are really going to travail for Zion, somehow or other you not only have to be in Zion but also on its walls.

What does that all mean? Well, let me put it as simply as I can. These watchmen have their own experience of Zion, and of the king within its gates. They have their own experience. They are under government. They are under His lordship. They hear His Word. They do His bidding. They are there in fellowship with Him. They have their own experience of Zion. They know what it is to be part of the building up of Zion like in Nehemiah's day. They had, as it were, a gun in one hand and a spade in the other. It was not quite like that; I think they had the sword in one hand, and a trowel in the other, but you know what I mean—a gun in one hand and a spade in the other. I have seen it many times in Israel today—a gun over the shoulder and a spade getting on with the job.

The point is that watchmen are not only watching but they are committed. They have their own experience of the building up and recovery of Zion. They know the difficulties about stone being built to stone, the whole difficulty of buildings going up in relation to one another, the whole city being a compact city; they have their own experience. They know something about the foundation. It says in Isaiah 28:16, "I have placed in Zion, a sure foundation, a tried stone." Of course, the apostle Peter brought this up and said, "Behold, I lay in Zion, a chief cornerstone" and it is all to do with this house of the Lord (1 Peter 2:6). "Ye also, as living stones are built up together as a house in the Lord" (1 Peter 2:5).

Now, my point about all this is very simple and it is just this: if these ones are going to be watchmen on the walls of Zion, then they have to have their own experience of Zion. They must have their own experience of relationship with one another there. Do you understand? As living stones, they have their experience of the foundation. You know, it is one thing to be able to meet with people that you agree with, but it is another thing when you have to find a foundation when there are people you do not exactly like or people you clash with temperamentally. It is much easier to say, "I feel the Lord's leading me off to the Baptists, or I feel that the Lord might be leading me off to the Methodists; I feel I have a job to do there." It is much easier to depart that way. Do you see? We gloss it up.

I have never known anybody to leave simply because they dislike somebody else, but I will tell you this, 75% to 80% of those who leave any company normally leave through personal collisions. There are people in the leadership or people elsewhere, people in responsibility, or just someone that they are having to share with and they cannot get on with them. They just cannot face the fact that they cannot get on with them and say, "I just cannot get on with So-and-So." No, they gloss it all up in spiritual terms. They say the Lord spoke to them in their quiet time. It is time for them to move, and on they have trotted. But they never get anywhere because they jump out of the frying pan and into the fire, normally. You see, the problem that God was trying to get you through on is a problem that is in *you*, not in the other person. If God could use that other difficult person to bring this whole problem in you out into the open and slay it and deal with it … well, it is a wonderful thing. You would be very thankful, wouldn't you? Instead of running off somewhere else, face the whole thing, and come through it. That is wonderful! Well, there we are.

These watchmen have their own experience of the battles and the joys of Zion. They are not just people who have been positioned on the walls, who have nothing whatsoever to do with the city. They have come through (if you know what I mean), from being bellboy right up through the whole firm, until in the end, they have this position of very real responsibility and authority to guard and watch.

The fellowship of the Lord is very wonderful in this matter because He says, "Ye that are the Lord's remembrancers, take ye no rest and give Him no rest." Now we have the second word: "Do not be silent," and do not let Him be still. So, the best way of translating it is just as we have. Take no rest and give Him no rest. Do not be quiet yourself and do not let Him be quiet. That is how you would probably put it if you understood it from the modern Hebrew. What a command!

Now the question immediately arises, if our Lord is all-powerful, and knows all things anyway, and works all things according to the counsel of His own will, why does He have to be reminded? I love how the ASV says, "Ye that are the Lord's remembrancers."

The Hebrew probably means *you who are there to remind the Lord*, but I think this is lovely, "the Lord's remembrancers." But why should we need to remind the Lord? He should surely not need to be reminded. He ought to know what He is doing. Why does He need to be reminded? Do you not think it is something to do with real fellowship?

Let me just for a moment take one digression on this matter because I believe it is very important. You know, it is so interesting in the whole matter of the kingdom of God being advanced, the will of God being done, and the work of the Lord being fulfilled that we have certain promises. For instance, in II Corinthians 1:20, "For how many soever be the promises of God, in Christ is the yes, and through Him is the Amen, to the glory of God." Now, can I just explain something to you? We just take this wonderful Word and say, "Oh wonderful! Wonderful! 'How many soever be the promises of God, in Christ is the yes, and through Him the Amen.' Isn't that marvellous? Standing on the promises of God."

But just wait. I think that first of all we need to see that the promises of God in Christ, however many there are, are yes, but "through Him the amen," is the problem. Do you understand what I am trying to say? I am trying to say that when we know that the will of God is to do this, this, and this, we get a promise made real to us by the Holy Spirit as a company of God's people, and immediately we know, "it is yes." It is yes, but our problem is the amen. It is one thing to have the yes, but *through* Christ, not in, "through Him the amen." In other words, you can get the yes, but it is the process by which the yes becomes fact, that works out the amen. You see, when we say "amen," we say "let it be, even so." I link this up with Hebrews 6:12: "Do not be sluggish, but be imitators of them who through faith and patience inherit the promises." In other words, faith may say, "It is yes," but patience is the only thing that can wait for the "amen." It is the final outworking of the promise.

Let me explain and illustrate. God told them, "Wheresoever the soul of your foot treads upon, that will I give you" (Joshua 1:3). The moment they put their feet down into the River Jordan onto the riverbed, what happened? There was an earthquake, or something else, up at the city, Adam. Immediately the waters were piled up and the people went over as on dry ground. It happened instantly. They did not wait. They probably had to wait an hour for the riverbed to really dry so they could go over, but I mean, what is an hour? It has all happened in a moment. It was absolutely marvellous. Here was the promise of the Lord, we would say, in Christ, "yes" and through Him, "amen." First came the "yes." They put their feet down in the water, it stopped, and then through Him, the "amen." Within hours, the whole nation was across into the promised land.

When they came to Jericho, they put their feet down, but what happened? If anyone had been a legalist they might have said, "Now listen everybody, God is all-powerful. We do not need to go round and round this city. All we need to do is to put our feet down one time and claim it in the name of the Lord. If the walls do not come down, something is wrong." Yet they had to go round those walls once a day for six days and seven times on the seventh day, and only on the seventh time did the walls come down. Is that not interesting? They had to have patience for seven days (Joshua 6).

What about Jerusalem? They could have taken it, yet they did not. Do you know how long it took for them to take Jerusalem? It was 400 years. It took 400 years before King David put his feet down, and the "amen" came. Now, what I am just trying to say is this: we need patience.

You see, in this whole ministry of intercession, we are given promises about certain things. Then if they do not happen immediately, we tend to get discouraged and what do we do? We very easily can fall to infighting. We can start on a kind of witch hunt. Someone is wrong. So-and-So is wrong. This is wrong. That is wrong. The other is wrong. We should not have done this. We should not have done that. Oh, the Devil loves it. He loves it. Everyone starts looking at one another. I am not saying there are not times when we need to clean up a whole lot of things amongst us and get things right, but you know, I have lived long enough, and am long enough in the tooth now to have seen some amazing things. I have seen the Lord bless, and then a bit later when there has been a hold up, someone has said, "If this and this was removed, we would get the blessing." The funny thing is that it was there when the blessing came before. In other words, although I am quite sure there are times when we have to really deal with things, particularly when the Lord reveals it to us, may God preserve us from witch hunts. It is quite a different thing when the Lord reveals Himself and unveils Himself, and then we all get right because we know in our hearts there is something wrong in us. It is an altogether different thing when we all start looking at one another, trying to put one another right. I say that this is very important, because there are times when it takes a moment, there are times when it takes seven days, and there are times when it takes 400 years. When the set time comes, the "amen" comes, but oh, for patience to battle on!

Daniel must have at times felt like giving up, especially when he was in the lion's den. There must have been times when He thought "Well, you know, the Lord said 70 years and somehow or other we are near to the end of the 70 years, and it is just getting darker and darker and darker and darker." He might have thought, "Why doesn't the Lord just do it?" No, the Lord gave him not only faith, but patience. Don't you think it is an interesting thing, dear ones, when Daniel really sought the Lord in Daniel 10:10–13? An angel came to him and touched him in such a way that he fell on the palms of his hands and on his knees, poor man. That was a powerful touch from heaven, like an electric shock. Then the angel said, "Daniel, the very first moment you started to pray, your prayer was heard and answered. And I have been sent, but I got delayed." What in the world could that mean: he got delayed? Then he says, "There was a fight between the Prince of Persia and the Prince of Greece." These princes are not earthly princes at all, they are spiritual principalities; they are not flesh and blood.

Take this question of the house in Jerusalem. My point is this: I have learned deeply that you cannot just say, "This, this, and this will happen," and it just happens. There are tremendous battles. Unless the Lord's people rise up to it, really take it through, and execute the will of God, then it is held up. Furthermore, the Lord *could* do it. With a flick of his fingers, He could just say, "It is done. It is done." But He does not. Why? Because He wants to teach us. It is as if He is saying, "Listen, if you are going to let Jerusalem remain in Jebusite control, it will remain under

Jebusite control. There is a big, strong man in charge of this city. You have been able to dislodge him out of the land, out of Jericho, out of Ai, but you cannot dislodge him out of Jerusalem. You need more." Do you understand? Now forgive this digression, but it is not really a digression at all, because it is all to do with this fellowship of the Lord.

There is only one explanation for why the Lord needs remembrancers. It is this: He wants to bring us into the place where we reign with Him in heavenly places, where we learn here and now in circumstances down here, what it is to bring the will of God into Richmond, what it is to bring the kingdom of God into Richmond, what it is to bring the kingdom of God into our circumstances, and what it is to bring them into the nation's circumstances. We have to learn it now. We are not going to learn it then; we have to learn it now. We have to learn that God gives us promises.

You would understand that there are times when I have heard promises given that I really do not think have been of the Lord, but there are other times, and many times, when the promises have been given of God, made to us by the Holy Spirit, and witnessed by two or three. Do you understand what I mean by two or three? In the mouth of two or three it has been established that this really is the Lord speaking, and then we have such a battle over its realisation. We wonder why the Lord does not come in. Then the whole danger can become fighting or witch hunting or whatever else. Let us see the Lord and get ourselves cleaned up and let holiness and righteousness come right into our lives, but let us remember that there are strong beings that have to be bound before we can spoil the strongman's goods. Until you and

I learn to do this intercession, we can only go so far. We are all the time taking this and taking that and yet somehow or other we never come to the point where actually the enemy is dislodged and we are through. May the Lord teach us this tremendous lesson.

Listen to what the Lord says in Isaiah 62:8–9, "The Lord had sworn by His right hand, by the arm of his strength, surely I will no more give thy grain to be food for thine enemies, foreigners shall not drink any new wine for which though hast laboured, but they that have garnered it shall eat it, and praise the Lord, and they that have gathered it shall drink it in the courts of my sanctuary." This is again, very interesting. What the Lord is saying is that there will be a harvest, only others will not get it, you will enjoy it. Oh, don't you think so much of Christian work is hard, hard work? Then, after all that comes the great disappointment, that those you have laboured for just go off? But the promise of the Lord here is that you will enjoy the harvest. They will not just go off—they will stay.

However, it is even more beautiful. You see, you never eat meals in the courts of the sanctuary, unless it is special meals. Did you know that? If you look into your Bible, you will find in the book of Exodus, in the book of Leviticus, the book of Numbers, certain laws given for meals that you can have in the temple courts. They were called peace offerings. Remember, when you brought in the new wine, then the priests and yourself could sit down and have a meal. It was a fellowship meal. What a lovely thought, that when the Lord has got His tithe, and when the Lord has got His offerings, you and the others sit down and enjoy it.

It is a beautiful thought for those of you who know your Bibles a little bit more.

The Challenge of the Lord

Let us go on finally to the last verses. If that is the fellowship of the Lord, His point is that in this Zion and Jerusalem, nothing will ever happen until He has those in fellowship with Him in His deepest of all ways in this whole ministry of intercession. Listen then to the challenge of the Lord in Isaiah 62:10: "Go through, go through the gates, Prepare ye the way of the people; cast up, cast up the highway; gather out the stones, lift up an ensign for the peoples." Now, we have got some very interesting things here. (Next time, we will be able to go on and really look at some of these things in-depth. For now, we will just underline and introduce them.) What does it mean "go through the gates"? Does it mean go through the gates to enter the city? Or does it mean go through the gates to cast up the highway? Well, it does not really matter, does it? Because what it means is *commit yourself.* That is all. Commit yourself to the life of Zion and to the children of Zion. Really commit yourself to the work of the Lord and to the purpose of the Lord in this matter.

First, you will have to commit yourself by going into the city through the gates. That is where the elders sit. Now, I am not saying anything about the elders, but what I mean is this: it means that you come under authority. You commit yourself. It is not just that you do what you think is right. You commit yourself to the community of God's people and come under authority. It is as simple as that. Once you have committed yourself to go in, you are going to go back out before long to prepare a way for the people, to cast up a highway, to gather out the stones.

Have you ever seen a big highway being prepared? It really is interesting, especially in stony, rocky country. You see all these men working like ants, slowly levelling away. First come the surveyors. (I am no engineer, so understand that if I am saying it all wrong.) But you get these men with all their funny little gadgets working. First of all, it looks like virgin soil to me. I have often seen them, not only here, but especially in Israel. I mean, you just spot it and think, "Something is going to happen here." Sure enough, a few months later, you start to see the first outline. Then before long, those great boulders all have been moved out of the way. It is tremendous.

What does it all really mean? Well, first of all, you have got to commit yourself. I wonder if you really are committed. You know, do not ever deceive yourself into thinking that you just do not agree with this or do not agree with that, because in the end, this matter of committing yourself to the Lord is a question of his lordship. It is as simple as that. Once you and I have really owned the lordship of Jesus, we will commit ourselves—no problem. We only have problems with our brothers and sisters—afraid of their clammy hands upon us and what they might do to manipulate us—when we have not owned the lordship of Jesus. Once we have the lordship of Jesus, we know He is bigger than they. "Go through the gates."

Here is the next thing: "prepare the way." There is a way to be prepared. Then, "casting up a highway." What does that mean? It is a way for people to come. There are many, many people that

God wants to bring to Zion, people who are not yet saved. Others who do know the Lord, but are in such afflicted and destitute circumstances, He wants to bring them, but there are boulders in the way. Some of those boulders are traditional, some of them are institutional, some of them are just our own bigoted prejudices. Some of them are blemishes in our church gatherings; things that really put other people off. It is maybe just a coldness we have towards people. We just do not welcome them. We do not smother them with love, if you know what I mean. We do not seem to warm up to the stranger amongst us. These can be boulders.

Everyone knows what it is like to come into a company where no one really takes an interest in you, where no one goes out of their way. You have lots of people all sitting there waiting for somebody else to talk to them. The British are incredible in this manner. I mean, it is a British disease. It really is. I am not trying to be funny; it is a British disease. You just do not get it in other places. In some other places you have to shake everybody's hand when you come in and shake everybody's hand before you go out. You know the kind I mean. Well, I know that can become a dreadful routine too, but at least it means that you have touched everybody. In other places, you get crushed to death in brothers' arms that nearly break your ribs. You know, smothered! I mean, it is not considered to be the least bit ungodly, but at least there is some kind of contact and you feel at least you are wanted. The British do suffer from this terrible inhibition not quite knowing what to do. The best idea ever is shoving a cup of tea in people's hands (especially the men), because when they have something in their hands, they seem as if they can then start to talk more normally. But you know, some of these can be stones.

We need to think about them. They are actual stones of stumbling. Someone may come in who is in great need and they have been overlooked. Everyone is busy talking with one another, the people they already know, and someone who is in real need comes in and goes out … and that is that and it is not always the unsaved.

Well, those are just small things, but there are many others—stones that are in the way. They are just stones of stumbling. You cannot have a highway where you have rocks littering the way. They have to be taken out. Now, isn't it an interesting thing that our Lord does not say, "I will go through the gates. I will prepare the way for the people. I will cast up the highway. I will gather up the stones. I will lift up the ensign for the peoples." What is an ensign? An ensign is a flag of the nation, or regiment, or whatever it is, a Royal Standard. It flies at a certain time, particularly in battle so that if any soldier or any unit gets separated from the commander, they can immediately look and see the ensign and know where he is. They know where their ranks are. Well, we need an ensign, don't we? In this battle people sometimes get separated. They get scattered. Then they do not know where they are. We need an ensign.

Well, the Lord does not say, "I will lift up the ensign." He says, "You must go through the gates. You must prepare the way for the people. You must cast up the highway and gather out the stones and lift up an ensign for the peoples." Oh, that the Lord would help us in this matter. It is one thing to talk about Zion. It is one thing to talk about the purpose of the Lord. It is another thing to get down to the actual hard work that is involved in the service of God if the salvation of Jerusalem and of Zion is to go forth as a lamp that burns, as a torch that burns.

Are you concerned about this? I am. Are you? Do you really want to be in this? The most wonderful thing in the whole wide world will be to meet the Lord when He comes and to be able to know that by the grace of God, with all our faults and weaknesses and failings, we were involved by His grace in this whole work that is on His heart. May God give you that burden and may He bring you to the place where there is a spiritual capacity for intercession and for really being with Him. Shall we bow together in prayer?

Lord, we have talked about Zion and the travail for Zion. Lord, we are very glad that this travail is not our travail; it is Thy travail. Lord, it is a travail that Thou canst bring into our spirits by Thy Holy Spirit. Lord, we pray, because we need divine illumination on a matter like this, wilt Thou take what has been said and really write it on our hearts, Lord. Let light be given on a number of things, oh Lord, in our way individually and in our way corporately. Lord, we pray that in some very real way for our locality, that Thy righteousness will go forth as brightness and Lord, Thy salvation as a torch that burns. Dear Lord, we need it in this town. Thou knowest all the unhappiness and sin and emptiness and aimlessness. Thou knowest, Lord, all the need amongst us who are born of Thy Spirit. Dear Lord, do this work we pray. We ask it together with thanksgiving, in the name of our Lord Jesus. Amen.

4.
The Work of Zion

Isaiah 62:1

For Zion's sake, will I not hold my peace and for Jerusalem's sake, I will not rest until her *righteousness go forth as brightness, and her salvation as a lamp, that burneth.*

We have ranged over a number of scriptures, both in the Psalms as well as in Isaiah on this whole matter of Zion. I am afraid that for many people, Zion is an old-fashioned word that we find in Sankey type hymns, or which we see engraved upon rather grey drab stone buildings, especially in the Welsh Valleys. Therefore, for some reason or another, we almost have some sort of odd notion, some strange idea about Zion. Yet when we really look at the Word it is amazing, because we find that there is a tremendous amount about Zion in the Word right the way through the Bible.

We have talked about the battle over Zion. We have talked about the building of Zion. We considered something of the travail for Zion in this Isaiah 62. Zion is the name that God gave to that matter which is most precious to His heart. That is why He calls us "the Zion of the Holy One of Israel." He says in Psalm 132:13–14 in very well-known words, "For the Lord hath chosen Zion; He hath desired it for His habitation [or home]. This is my resting-place forever: here will I dwell ..."

Now, we saw in Psalm 2 that there were three things about that Psalm. First of all, you had the king. "Yet have I set My king ..." All the nations are raging and the peoples are imagining vain things, and the kings and rulers are setting themselves against the Lord and His anointed. But the Lord says, "Yet I have set My King." That is the first thing, the King. The second thing is this: "Yet have I set My King upon My holy hill of Zion," or "upon Zion, the mountain of My holiness," as it is literally in Hebrew. The third thing is: "... the uttermost parts of the earth for His possession."

I wish we could talk more about the uttermost parts of the earth coming back to the Lord, the restitution of all things. What a wonderful subject! Almost at the beginning of the Bible, right in the first books of the Bible, we have this wonderful word: "The Lord said, 'but as truly as I live, the earth shall be filled with the glory of God,'" (Numbers 14:21). Then in another place, it comes not once, but two or three times, "And the earth shall be filled with the knowledge of the glory of God, as the waters cover the sea" (Isaiah 11:9). Then, the Psalmists speak about that day using mostly, almost emotional language. They speak of trees clapping their hands, of fields exulting in joy, of hills and valleys singing the praise of God because something happens to the natural creation (see Psalm 98:8 and Isaiah 55:12).

Now, the heart of the whole matter is the King. Thank God He is the new man! He is the last Adam, and He is the new man. Then we have His Zion and that is the new man, too. Those who are born of God, Jerusalem which is above, which is free, which is the mother of us all. Those who have been born of God, they are in this Zion.

What is Zion? Every real believer is a true Zionist, at least spiritually, a spiritual Zionist, because you and I belong to a movement, a divine movement for world liberation. It is the liberation of this whole world, not only the peoples, not only the nations, not just individuals, but the very natural creation itself, the liberation of the whole earth back into the liberty of the glory of the sons of God. Well, it is a tremendous subject, but we must go on. We are just talking about the fact of Zion. We have looked at Zion, we have looked at what it means, and we have looked at some of the scriptures.

We come now to Isaiah 58. Here we have the work of Zion. Of course, you understand we are in Zion, and we are coming to Zion. Zion, as it were, is gloriously completed and yet it is being built. It is a wonderful paradox. We have all this travail for Zion, and yet we are watchmen on the walls of Zion, as it says in Isaiah 62. Now we have this word here. Let us read it from Isaiah 58:6–14.

Is not this the fast that I have chosen: to loose the bonds of wickedness, to undo the bands of the yoke, and to let the oppressed go free, and that ye break every yoke? Is it not to deal thy bread to the hungry, and that thou bring the poor that are cast out to thy house? when thou seest the naked, that thou cover him; and that thou hide not thyself on my own flesh? Then shall thy light break forth as the morning, and thy healing shall spring forth speedily; and thy righteousness will go before thee; the glory of the Lord shall be thy rearward. Then shalt thou call, and the Lord will answer; thou shalt cry, and he will say, Here I am.

If thou take away from the midst of thee the yoke, the putting forth of the finger, and speaking wickedly, and if thou draw out thy soul to the hungry and satisfy the afflicted soul, then shall thy light rise in darkness, and thine obscurity be as the noonday; and the Lord will guide thee continually, and satisfy thy soul in dry places, and make strong thy bones; and thou shall be like a watered garden, and like a spring of water, whose waters fail not. And they that shall be of thee shall build the old waste places; thou shalt raise up the foundations of many generations; and thou shall be called The repairer of the breach, The restorer of paths to dwell in.

If thou turn away thy foot from the sabbath, from doing thy pleasure on my holy day; and call the sabbath a delight, and the holy of the Lord honourable; and shalt honour it, not doing thine ways, nor finding thine own pleasure, nor speaking thine own words: then shalt thou delight thyself in the Lord; and I will make thee to ride upon the high places of the earth. And I will feed thee with the heritage of Jacob thy father: for the mouth of the Lord hath spoken it.

Previously, we ended considering these verses in Isaiah chapter 62 from verse 10: "Go through, go through the gates; prepare ye the way of the people; cast up, cast up the highway; gather out the stones; lift up an ensign for the peoples." The Lord has revealed here His determination, that He will not hold His peace, He will not be inactive. For Zion's sake, for Jerusalem's sake, He will not be silent or quiet, "until her righteousness go forth as brightness" (see verse one). *Clear shining after tempest* is that word. Her salvation, as a flaming torch, giving light to all who can see.

The Challenge of the Lord to Us

Then He said that He will not do this without the fellowship of His people. "I have set watchmen upon Thy walls, O Jerusalem; they shall never hold their peace day nor night: ye that are the Lord's remembrancers, take no rest, and give Him no rest, till He establish, and till He make Jerusalem a praise in the earth" (Isaiah 62:6–7).

Then comes the challenge. You belong to Zion. You have been saved by the King of Zion, through the Messiah. Through the Messiah King, you have come into the salvation of God, you have been brought into the kingdom of God, and you have been brought into the purpose of God. Here comes the challenge: commit yourself. Do not just dither. Do not just dither on the periphery, do not just be a spectator of things, do not just taste what you like and leave what you do not like, and just be sort of irresponsible. Commit yourself! Go through the gates. This can mean two things. It could mean to go through the gates into the city and commit yourself to the building of Zion, to the life of Zion, to all the battles and joys of Zion, to the ministry of intercession. Yet it can also mean that once you have gone in and committed yourself that way, now, go out and prepare a way for the people.

What does this mean to "prepare a way for the people"? What does it mean to "cast up a highway"? You notice the Lord does not say, "I will go through the gates. I will prepare the way for the people. I will cast up a highway. I will gather out the stones. I will lift up ..." No, no. He says, "You go through. You prepare the way for the people. You cast up a highway. You gather out the stones. You lift up an ensign for the peoples." There is a responsibility that we as the people of God have got.

Now, all of us know what a tragedy it has been. We cannot point a finger at any group of the Lord's people, but what a tragedy it has been in the history of the church, that no sooner does the Lord start to work and reveal things than we turn it all into a 'thing.' Then we just have a routine. Somehow or other we just go up and down and up and down and we never get to the real heart of the matter. We never get on with the job.

You know, it is entirely possible to see the purpose of God, to have a vision, in one sense, an understanding of what the Lord really wants, and yet to deceive ourselves into believing that in seeing it we are part of it. Whereas the challenge is to come right down to the practical level—the builder's yard—the cutting and the shaping, the being fitted together, the opening up to one another, the real heart sharing of our beings with one another. Oh, we do not like this. We find this very hard. We are so afraid that people are going to damage us, that people are going to manipulate us, that they are going to somehow or other tread over our sensitivities. I think there is indeed a likelihood that, to a certain extent, some of that could happen. However, you know the Lord will turn it all to good account. Does someone tread over your sensitivities? It is an opportunity to die to self.

People are always saying, "Oh, I wish I knew more deeply the way of the cross," yet as soon as the opportunity comes, they run a thousand miles. It is strange, is it not? We shall have plenty of opportunities of falling into the ground and dying in this whole matter of being committed to the building of Zion.

The Practical Things

If you turn to Isaiah 58, I believe that here we have some very practical and marvellous things. There is something which we have to do. What is the prophet speaking about in this incredible chapter? What the Lord is saying through the prophet Isaiah is this: "You seek Me daily," He says. "You fast, you put ashes on your head and spread-out sackcloth," but He said, "this is not the fast I want. Because in doing this very thing, you are escaping the real issue." He says to these people that first of all the real issue is "to loose the bonds of wickedness, to undo the bands of the yoke, to let the oppressed go free and that ye break every yoke" (verse 6).

Here is the second thing: "Deal thy bread to the hungry ... bring the poor that are cast out to thy house ... when thou seest the naked, cover him; and ... hide not thyself from thine own flesh" (verse 7).

Then thirdly: "Take away from the midst of thee the yoke, the putting forth of the finger, and speaking wickedly ... draw out thy soul to the hungry, and satisfy the afflicted soul" (verse 9–10a).

The fourth thing is this: "Turn away thy foot from the Sabbath, from doing thy pleasure on My holy day; and call the Sabbath a delight, and the holy of the Lord honourable; and honour it, not doing thine own ways, nor finding thine own pleasure, nor speaking thine own words" (verse 13).

The Promises

Now, the promises are just as marvellous. Each time the promise becomes more glorious than before. We have this promise in verse eight, "Then shall thy light break forth as the morning, and thy healing shall spring forth speedily." What a lovely promise that is: *the dawn of a new day*. It will be a new day, a new chapter, a new beginning, just like light coming out of darkness which brings hope to all men. Then healing, *speedily springing forth; recovery* is the way it puts it in the New American Standard. Oh, the need that there is amongst the people of God for recovery, the need that there is all round. Here, it is a promise.

Then, listen to this; He says, "... righteousness shall go before thee; and the glory of the Lord shall be thy rearward" (verse 8). Is that not wonderful? Justification going in front, so no need for the devil to unnerve you by saying, "Oh, you? You're nothing." Justification will go before you, and behind you will come the glory of the Lord. It is the right order. You will never know glory unless you have been justified. But if you have been justified, you will be glorified. What a wonderful thing! What a protection from all around! Who is this? It is the Lord, the Lord my righteousness, the Lord our righteousness, and the Lord our glory. You then hear this wonderful word, "Thou shalt call, and the Lord will answer; thou shalt cry and he will say, 'Here I am'" (verse 9).

Then, you have a second promise in verse 10: "Then shall my light rise in darkness, and thine obscurity be as the noonday."

It is beautifully put in the New American Standard: "Thy gloom shall be as midday." Is anyone gloomy? Lots of the Lord's people are gloomy. It says, "Thy gloom shall be as midday," no gloom at all. There is glorious light of the sun at midday.

Then, he goes on: "The Lord will guide thee continually, and satisfy thy soul in dry places" (verse 11). There are going to be many dry places in these days that lie ahead. If people are dependent upon our meetings in the years that lie ahead, consider that we have got dry places coming when persecution starts, when this antichrist begins to become visible and when the very atmosphere is filled with evil. We are seeing the beginning of those days now and there are dry places coming. Again, the word in Hebrew is *scorched places*; places that are absolutely waterless, and at such a temperature that you cannot breathe in them. Now what does the Lord say? He says He will satisfy thy soul in such places and He will make strong thy bones.

You know, bones are very important things. Did you know that? Once your bones begin to deteriorate your health deteriorates. I expect a number of you, especially older ones, know the trouble with bone crumbling or whatever you like to call it. I mean, in non-technical language, bones start to crumble; the marrow is not good anymore either. You have a lot of problems when that happens. Now, there is a lot of that amongst the Lord's people. If you look at them, they seem quite okay; only God knows their bones are crumbling. The heart of the whole matter that gives health to them is in danger. Now the Lord says, "Thy bones shall be strong." What a wonderful thing, strong bones, wonderful! It often says they are health to thy marrow, does it not? See? The Bible has got a lot to say about bones and marrow.

"Thou shall be like a watered garden, like a spring of water, whose waters fail not." What is the point? What is the point of having a lovely garden with a well in the centre of it and the whole thing with luscious greenery, full of the fragrance of flowers and full of fruit, if the waters fail? If the waters fail, the whole garden is gone. There is nothing you can do. The whole thing will die. The Lord says this is His promise if we are to take care of these other matters: "We shall be like a watered garden, like a spring of water, whose waters fail not" (verse 11).

Then He says, "They that shall be of thee shall build the old waste places; thou shalt raise up the foundations of many generations" (verse 12). What does that mean? It means not despising church history, but recovering every value in the history of the church. I am very sorry when I go around sometimes to see how some people just want to cut themselves off from anything that has gone before, as if all the history of the church means absolutely nothing to us in this new generation. We want to be absolutely novel thinking: "We are in something totally new. All the rest have failed, but we have not failed." This is a mistake. God has done some tremendous things in the history of the church and recovered vital truths. What a wonderful thing it is, if we are so walking with the Lord, that we have all of it like a great treasury. At the end of the age, should not the church be richer than any other phase in church history? We have behind us a tremendous number of battles won, truths recovered, and deeper experiences of the Lord known.

"Thou shall be called a repairer of the breach, the restorer of paths to dwell in" (verse 12). Some of you might wonder, how do you dwell in a path? I would not like that. I would not like to sort of sit in the highway with people travelling, going backwards and forwards. That does not seem to be a very pleasant place, but it doesn't mean that. It means you shall be the restorer of streets to dwell in.

Then you have this last promise in verse 14, the most wonderful of all, "Then shalt thou delight thyself in the Lord; and I will make thee to ride upon the high places of the earth; and I will feed thee with the heritage of Jacob, thy father." What a wonderful word that is as well: riding upon the high places of the earth. Oh, for an experience like that! I know many people who would love to delight in the Lord, but they cannot delight in the Lord. Do you know that to delight in the Lord is a gift? God does not respond to cheapness. To really delight in the Lord is something He gives. When we give Him His rights, then it is as if He gives us an especial way with Himself. We will look at that in the future, but it is just something to point out now: "to delight in the Lord."

The Chosen Fast

Now, would you just look at the first of these two things a little more in detail, because in actual fact, we have found this whole matter linked again and again. In Isaiah 61, we find that where it says "the Spirit of the Lord God is upon Me because the Lord hath anointed Me," immediately it goes on in verse four, "They shall build the old waste places; they shall raise up the former desolations." In other words, the breaking of the bondage, the binding up of the broken-hearted, the proclaiming of liberty to those who are in prison, and all these things, have a lot to do with the building of Zion.

Again, you will find it in Psalm 102. This is another Psalm we have looked at in these times, remember? In verse 13, "Thou wilt arise, and have mercy upon Zion; for it is time to have pity upon her, Yea, the set time has come." Now listen to what it says in verses 17 and 18, "He hath regarded the prayer of the destitute and hath not despised their prayer. This shall be written for the generation to come; and a people which shall be created shall praise the Lord." This is the Zion: a people that shall be created.

"Thy sons marrying thee" is the way it is put in Isaiah 62:5, "For He has looked down, from the height of His sanctuary from heaven did the Lord behold the earth to hear the sighing of the prisoner, to loose those that are appointed to death, that men may declare the name of the Lord in Zion." This whole matter of really tackling some of these practical questions is very much related to the building of Zion and the completion of Zion. In other words, it is the realisation of the purpose of God.

If you will notice them very carefully, there are four things here in Isaiah 58:6: "Is not this My chosen fast?" (This is the chosen fast of the Lord.) Here they are:

(1)   loose the bonds of wickedness
(2)   undo the bands of the yoke
(3)   let the oppressed go free
(4)   break every yoke

Now, this had particular reference in Isaiah's day to slavery. Although the people of God were allowed to buy slaves that were not children of Israel, the one thing they were forbidden was to have a Hebrew slave. If you look at this, you will find it in Leviticus 25:39, "If thy brother be waxed poor with thee, and sell himself unto thee; thou shalt not make him to serve as a bondservant [a slave, or a bond slave]. As a hired servant, and as a sojourner, he shall be with thee; he shall serve with thee unto the year of Jubilee." In other words, if someone who is Hebrew, Jewish, were to come and say, "Look, I'm so poor, I want to sell myself to you so that I can pay for my family," and so on, you can only take him on as a hired servant with wages. You cannot buy him as a slave.

Now, this is what Isaiah was really talking about in the first instance. When he said to the people of God, "If you want to see the salvation of Zion going forth as a burning torch, a flaming torch to the ends of the earth, if you want to see the righteousness of Jerusalem as brightness, then you must loose the bonds of wickedness. You must undo the bands of the yoke. You must let the oppressed go free. You must break every yoke."

Now this word is interesting: *bonds of wickedness*, because the Hebrew root is "to bind or twist powerfully." Then it came to mean bonds or fetters or pangs—the pangs of wickedness. I find that most expressive because I always find that the bonds of wickedness lead to the pangs of wickedness. Dear people of God, are we not surrounded by a whole community that is in the bonds of wickedness? It is not always their fault. They have been born into something. They have got a poison in their bloodstream and the enemy has taken them captive at his will. He does with them just what he wants. He puts into their minds the ideas he wants and he leads them in the way that he wants them to go.

Oh, dear ones, our job is to proclaim the liberty of the Lord. The Lord Jesus said, "The Spirit of the Lord God is upon me." What has He come to proclaim? He has come to proclaim liberty to those that are captives, the opening of the prison to those that are in fetters," and so on.

Now you know, we have a job here. In this word *bands of the yoke* or of the *leather thongs*, the actual word *yoke* here is the pole that goes across. Then the leather thongs bind the two poor animals to it, either one or two. He says we are to undo those thongs that bind people to that yoke.

Then he speaks of, "Let the oppressed go free." It is a very interesting word. It means those that are crushed, those that are shattered. Now, do you notice it is all in general terms here? He does not speak of bringing them into *thy* house, or dealing out *thy* bread or taking out from the midst of *thee*. This is general. It is as if God puts His finger upon the whole situation in the world and says, there can be no Zion until there is a people who are so built together in the Lord, so experiencing the salvation and the power of the Lord, that they can then begin to minister to the world. They can go out in service to the world and they can proclaim liberation for the captives. It is the heart of the matter.

Satan's great weapon is bondage. It says in Hebrews 2:14b–15, that the Lord "might deliver all them who through fear of death were all their lifetime subject to bondage." This is the enemy's great weapon, and it is not only here that we find it. Oh, anyone here who knows anything about the service of God abroad, you know just what I am talking about.

Now, I want to tell you something. There used to be days when we were in Egypt and elsewhere where you could almost tangibly feel the darkness. I remember there were times when I tried to pray when it was as if some hand almost came around one's throat. Many servants of the Lord will tell you that in India, or in Indonesia, or in many of these parts of the earth there is a sense of darkness, of bondage in the very atmosphere when you try to pray. Do you remember how James Fraser could not get through? In the end, the thought came into his heart that he would go up onto the highest mountain in Lisuland, and shout at the top of his voice—north, south, east and west: "Jesus Christ is Lord." When he did that … the break came. The first Lisu family to turn to the Lord, turned to the Lord. It is a tangible thing.

I want to tell you something else. Each time one comes back to this country, one senses a little bit more of that bondage in the atmosphere. That is why we are having a greater battle in prayer and we are going to have a greater and greater battle. Our whole country now has gone back to paganism, and with it all other kinds of things, and into the atmosphere comes this bondage. Now, you and I, we have a job to do or we are never going to see Zion built. Do you honestly think we are just going to see Zion built? I mean, we can go out, we can testify, we can go from house to house, we can go and do coffee bar work, we can have evangelistic meetings, but we all know that we can do all these things but nothing happens. Why does nothing happen—all the work, all the endeavour, even the prayer? It is because unless we get behind the scenes to loose the bonds of wickedness, to undo the bands of the yoke, we can never let the oppressed go free. It is an amazing fact that once we start to really learn this lesson, things begin to happen.

Now this bondage covers everything, whether it is the unsaved world or the people of God. Don't you think our greatest problem as the people of God is bondage? It is not just bondage to bad habits. Sometimes it is bondage to tradition. Sometimes it is a terrible inhibition. Sometimes it is some kind of complex, which has settled on us and we cannot get free from it.

I think that this is a tremendous command of our Lord to us to face this whole matter. He has most certainly dealt with it. You know the kind of thing; I can tell you from my own experience. People sometimes come to me and say, "For the last month or two I have so wanted to do this and this and I can't." Sometimes it is just a matter of expressing a bit of love to somebody, and they cannot do it. I wonder if that is the experience of anybody reading this. For instance, you really want to contribute in praise; you really would love to, and you just cannot. It is as if there is something in the atmosphere which says "No, this shall not be."

Now, I know it myself. I know what it is sometimes to sit there and feel that the Lord wants us to do a certain thing. Then I immediately become afraid of everybody else and think, "Well, they'll think I'm a nutcase if I get up and say this, and this, and this." Everyone thinks, "Oh, one of the leaders, I mean, if they get up, of course, everything is different." But it is amazing. It is something almost in the atmosphere, as if you cannot be free to do the will of God. As if it says to you, "Don't you lift your hands up. What do you think they're all going to think of you? Suggest that they shake hands with one another? What do you think you're doing? It will be the end! You will embarrass them." So you just sit there. The interesting thing is this: no one knows what is going on in one's heart, but an atmosphere of heaviness settles upon the whole gathering and the whole work. Now, we don't want that kind of freedom which is license, where people just do all kinds of weird things because they say they are free. God preserve us from that kind of freedom. However, we do need the freedom to do the will of God. We really do need the freedom to do the will of God. When we know that we should do this or that—just to love each other, just to care for each other, just to express concern for one another.

It is amazing to me when someone comes to me and says, "I have had this concern for So-and-So for a whole month," and they have never voiced it. When you say, "Well, why on earth didn't you say something?"

"Well, I just felt I couldn't!"

To me, that is bondage. Now, I am not saying that we now have got to lay hands on everybody, you know that kind of almighty deliverance ministry, and say, "We will now start upon every one of you one by one, and go through you all ..."

I mean, very much of this bondage is in the atmosphere. It is not anything to do with the company of believers here involved. Indeed, I would say very much more than this. I would say that if the Lord is amongst us, we shall know this bondage there in the atmosphere all the time, unless it is resisted in the name of the Lord because the enemy is always present where the Lord is present. He is there to somehow alienate the people of God from the Lord, to somehow bring a kind of dampening, heavy influence upon the whole, to stop real worship, to stop real prayer, to stop real ministry, to stop anything from really coming through. So, I say that this whole matter of our loosing the bonds of wickedness, undoing the bands of the yoke, letting the oppressed go free, and breaking every yoke is very, very important indeed. It has got to be a part of an ongoing ministry.

The Practical Side: Praise and Intercession

On the practical side, how can we do this? Well, there are one or two ways. We have got to always be careful of everything so that it does not become a rote thing or a method, but one way is to praise the Lord. Have you noticed that whenever we really praise the Lord, that atmosphere of bondage recedes? Always.

Another way is by intercession. Now I say intercession, not just prayer, but intercession. There is no way to deal with bondage in the atmosphere or in the life of a church except by taking action in the place of prayer. It is not just saying, "Lord, free us, Lord, do this," but announcing that we are the freed people of God, that we are in the freedom of Christ wherewith He has made us free.

What does the Word say? It is very interesting. Listen to Galatians 5:1: "For freedom, did Christ set us free. Stand fast, therefore, and be not entangled again, in a yoke of bondage?" Did you hear that? Stand fast, be strong, stand in this freedom. Do not just think it is going to be there today because you were freed and liberated ten years ago. No, not at all. If you are the Lord's child, you can be sure that the enemy is out to bind you and he will put a thong and another thong and another thong, and he will bind you to a yoke. It means you will have to go that way of the yoke and the yoke will be very heavy on you. It will cause sores. So you see, we have a job to do here.

The Practical Side: By Truth

Another way in which bondage is destroyed is by truth. It is so simple when it comes to it—the proclamation and declaration of truth. Why do we often assert that Jesus is Lord? It is because that is truth. It is when there is that declaration of truth that something happens in the unseen. You know, when we have a time of ministry and a real truth comes under anointing, the whole atmosphere is cleansed. Have you noticed it? I have seen it again and again. It is as if you are clean through the word which the Lord has spoken to you. It is as if a whole cleansing comes into the air, as if by the very proclamation of truth something happens. I notice it in towns where they have a history of the preaching of the gospel; there is an atmosphere in the streets which is freer because the truth itself has effect. Do not despise truth. Do not despise preaching. Do not despise the ministry of God's Word, because the enemy and all that invisible host that watches, know very well when it is truth. Truth has a tremendous effect upon it all.

The Practical Side: More Examples

Then, of course, there are many other ways: executive action, for example. There are times when we have to lay hands on one another in the name of the Lord and declare that a person is free. That is wonderful, isn't it? Many of you have known what it is to have someone minister to you in the name of the Lord, and to declare that you are free and you know it; you are free. Something has broken inside.

Is it not wonderful about baptism? Again and again, I have seen people in the waters of baptism come out and some fetter has just been snapped in the waters of baptism. It is extraordinary. All these things are all part of this ongoing ministry. We need to care for one another in this matter.

Of course, evangelism is another way. By going out, taking the whole thing onto the offensive, we go out and we proclaim the Lord. We proclaim the salvation of the Lord and the ascension and authority of the Lord.

The surest way you and I can be in this matter of freedom is to hold fast the Head. If I really hold fast the Head, I shall be free, because it says, "If the Son shall make you free, ye shall be free indeed" (John 8:36). So, when I really have a living experience of the Lord, I am free. For where the Spirit of the Lord is, there is liberty. Don't we all know this as a continual battle? It would be lovely to think that we could just leave it. I want to tell you something. Bondage is not something that just leaves you static. When the enemy binds a person or a company, it is progressive. The end is always the destruction and subjugation of that person or that company to the enemy's will and mind. Never forget that. That is why, if you know any bondage in your life and heart, you need to really start looking to the Lord: "Deal with this thing, Lord." Let us all rise up together and help one another in this matter, that we may be the freed people of the Lord, not only freed from Egypt, but also Egypt out of us. It is a wonderful thing when we really can walk with the Lord in this matter and let Him do it.

The Personal Application

There is one other thing I want to just underline and that is Isaiah 58:7. "Deal thy bread to the hungry, ... bring the poor that are cast out to thy house, when thou seest the naked, that thou cover him; ... hide not thy self from thine own flesh."

"Deal thy bread to the hungry." That is interesting, isn't it? You will notice straightaway that this is not general like the first; this is all to do with you and me. Deal *thy* bread to the hungry, when *thou* seest the naked that *thou* cover him. Bring the poor that is cast out into *thy* house, hide not *thyself* from *thine* own flesh.

It has all gone to a much more personal level, hasn't it? It has come to us now. The first thing was general, the whole weapon of the enemy against us, and indeed against the Lord in this world. Now it comes home to us.

What is this whole matter? Surely, I could cover it by saying it means love and compassion in all relationships. I think we have to remember that there are times when we ought to deal our bread physically. I mean, the New American Standard Bible says, "Share thy bread." Well, I think it is about time we woke up to this. It is all very well to talk about the building up of Zion, but there are some people who have never ever exercised hospitality, hardly with anybody.

What does the Word of God say? It says in Hebrews 13:2, "Forget not to show love unto strangers, for thereby some have entertained angels unawares." Think of that. Sometimes we only have very close friends come to our home. What a wonderful thing it is to have a stranger come to our home and share a meal with them. Share your bread with them. Has God given you a home? Has God given you bread? Has God given you some kind of income? Share it. Do not hold it to yourself. If you do, you will have multitudes of troubles. It is always the same. Hold to yourself your things, and you will have problem after problem. Share, and the Lord will take responsibility for you. There is great joy in sharing. You will get some difficult people. You will also get angels unawares. Isn't it best to put up with ten difficult people if you get the angel unawares at the end? I mean, think! It might all be a training ground, but finally, you have got the angel. What a blessing sometimes it can be. Someone you have taken into your home, in the end, becomes such a blessing to you and your family and to all of us. "Deal thy bread to the hungry."

Or again, I think of it what it says in James 2:14–16, "What did it profit my brethren if a man say he have faith, but have not works, can that faith save him? If a brother or sister be naked and in lack of daily food, and one of you tell them, 'Go in peace, be ye warmed and filled ...'" That means, "Praise the Lord," said with a slap on the back. We all do this, don't we? Someone is in desperate need; they may not have brought it out into the open. But we are not even sensitive to the Lord, at least for the promptings of the Spirit to tell us there is someone in need. Now we just say, "Praise the Lord." What we have said is, "Go in peace, be warmed and filled," and notwithstanding we give them nothing.

What does the Word say? "What does it profit?" it says. If you give them not the things needful to the body, what does it profit? You may pray for somebody's spiritual increase, and they are dying of starvation. Well, we need not only to pray for their spiritual increase, and so on, we need to care for them, as well, in a practical manner. Now, all these things have so much to tell us.

In Romans 12:13, you have the same thing again. It says, "... communicating to the necessities of the saints, given to hospitality." This word *communicating* is an old-fashioned word, which really means giving your money. It is a nice old word. Some of you may prefer to leave it as a nice old word, but actually, what it means is sharing your cash with the saints. Communicating.

It is exactly the same when you find it again in Galatians 6:6: "Let him that is taught in the Word communicate unto Him that teacheth in all good things." It does not mean communicate, as in, you go up afterwards and say, "That was a wonderful word." Then you think, "Boy, I have communicated with him. That's good." It does not mean that. It means you share your money. It is very practical, isn't it? We are not meant just to just look at one another in a kind of spiritual way, and never do anything for one another. We are to share our bread with the hungry; care for one another. There is a lot to this.

"Bring the poor that is cast out into thy house ... cover the naked." You see, it is not only the physical side, the natural side, there is the spiritual side, too. We are surrounded with people that are hungry. We have been greatly blessed in this company of believers with much that the Lord has given us, but we are surrounded on all sides by the people of God who are in terrible hunger.

Years ago, I asked a dear servant of the Lord: "What do you think will be the end of this pouring out of the Holy Spirit, this charismatic experience all over the earth?"

He said, "In ten years' time, there will come a cry for teaching and for the Word of God such as we have never seen in our lifetime."

This is exactly what has happened. This moving of the Holy Spirit has produced a hunger in the people of God and everywhere, everywhere, everywhere we have experience, but we have no teaching! We need teaching as well. We need to be deeply taught. We need to share what we have of the Lord. Has the Lord given us spiritual bread? Let us share our spiritual bread. Thank God for practical things such as the tapes ministry, which seem to be so technical and yet what a lot is done through that! We hear of lives that have met with God and little groups that have come into something more. It is a sharing of our bread. We need so much to look at these kinds of things. The people who are poor, that are cast out—there are many amongst the Lord's people who are afflicted, who are destitute, who are lonely—we need to care for them.

"Hide not thy self from thine own flesh." What does that mean? If you turn to Deuteronomy 22:1–4, you will find that it is actually mentioned: "Thou shalt not see thy brother's ox or his sheep go astray, and hide thyself from them: thou shalt surely bring them again unto thy brother. And if thy brother be not nigh unto thee, or if thou know him not, then thou shalt bring it home to thy house, and it shall be with thee until thy brother seek after it, and thou shalt restore it to him. And so shalt thou do with his ass; and so shalt thou do with his garment; and so shall thy do with every lost thing of thy brother's, which he hath lost, and thou hast found: thou mayest not hide thyself. Thou shalt not see thy brother's ass or his ox fallen down by the way, and hide thyself from them: thou shalt surely help him to lift them up again." How practical the Word of God is!

What does it mean "hide thyself"? It just means this: you do not want to know. This has a very real relationship to our own families. I know people who are the Lord's, who will never do a single thing in their family; they will never help. They don't want to know. If there is a ceiling that needs to be to be painted, they don't want to know. If there is a practical job that ought to be done, they don't want to know. Now, anyone who does not care for his own household is worse than an unbeliever, Paul says in the second letter to Timothy. So, we must first care for our own flesh. "Honour thy father and thy mother all the days of thy life," it says (see Exodus 20:12). There are many other things about our relationships to children, to husband, to wife, and to family. We have to take real notice of all these things. We must not hide ourselves. You see, much of life is spent just not wanting to know something. We say that what the eye doesn't see, the heart doesn't grieve over.

Some might wonder why this word is given in Deuteronomy. It says, if you see your brother's ox, or ass, and so on, you have got to go and catch the wretched thing. Have you ever tried to catch an ass? I mean, oxen and ass are not the easiest of things to really get hold of once they have gone astray. Now, I can imagine a farmer with a busy life is always saying, "Oh, that stupid brother of mine. Why didn't he keep his own animals under control? Why should I spend the whole day having to leave my farm while I go round and try to find this and that and the other?"

But it says, "Thou shalt not hide thyself." If you see his ox fallen into a ditch—you know how big an ox is—can you imagine it? Fallen into a ditch! You shall help him lift it up. He cannot do it alone. There is the poor man straining; he cannot get it. So, you go and give him a hand. It may take hours out of your time schedule, but you have got to do it. Hide not thyself from thine own flesh. Did you realize this is part of the building of Zion?

You see, it is very easy to be sort of all like 'Marys' and no 'Marthas'. We know the Lord said Mary has chosen the better part, sitting at His feet adoringly. However, sometimes I feel some people would like to sit at the Lord's feet adoringly while there are a thousand and one things to which they ought to be attending. Zion is not going to be built by people sitting at our Lord's feet adoringly, unless hand in hand, a lot of practical things get done as well. We can forget that there is a world in bonds of wickedness all around us, that has the bands of the yoke upon them, that are crushed and shattered. Somehow or other, we have not only to say, "Lord, please do something," we have got to take action in the name of the Lord. We have a spiritual authority over the area. We have a spiritual authority in the name of Jesus to break the bondage and the power of the enemy in these lives, and in the community in which God has placed us.

In the same way it is here, with this matter of love and compassion. We are to care for one another, not only physically, but spiritually. We are to share what God has given us. We are not to hide ourselves from our own flesh. Love and compassion are the key to all true service and there is no better way to prepare a way for the people or to gather out the stones. There are many boulders that have tripped up many people in the world, and many young believers who wanted to come into the things of God, have tripped on these boulders. They have made the going difficult for them, and we are to blame. Why are we to blame? Because we should have taken the boulders out of the way, gathered out the stones. How do we prepare the way? We prepare a way by love and compassion. I wonder whether that comes home to you as it comes home to me.

You know, it is interesting that the Apostle Paul said, in Galatians 5:1, "For freedom did Christ set us free, Stand fast therefore, and be not entangled again in a yoke of bondage." Then he says in verse 13, "For ye brethren, were called for freedom. Only use not your freedom for an occasion to the flesh, but through love be servants, one of another." Now here you have, interestingly enough, the two things that we have in Isaiah 58.

First, liberation, freedom. Secondly, love, loving service. Through love, be servants one of another.

Do you want to see Zion built? Then dear friends, if we are really going to see this, and we are in the day when our Lord will return, and this work is going to be completed, we need also to understand a little bit about the ministry of Zion. The first thing is this matter of bondage. It would be a very interesting thing to me to know how many of you feel you have an area of bondage in your life. It would be very interesting. I reckon that about two-thirds of us would say that we do, because we know there are areas of bondage. Now listen, we need to open up to one another on these things.

It is two-sided. One side is the house of God, really caring and moving out, but the other side is yourself. How can every yoke be broken if people do not come out into the open? Then again, sometimes people can be free, but they will fall back, because somehow or other they expect to be carried. They will not themselves walk in the Spirit. Do you understand? So, they will fall back again. There are many, many problems in this whole matter, but if it could only be two-sided: on the one side, we, caring for one another and going out to one another, and on the other side, our opening up of ourselves to one another, and coming out into the open. After all, if there is a bondage, if there is a limitation, if there is an inhibition, and if it really is hindering the Lord's work in your life, then through you, in the family, isn't it best to come out into the open? Just say, "Could you pray for me? I have a need here." In so doing, we face reality, and we get to know each other; we get to love each other. When people come out into the open you cannot help it, your heart goes out to them. If you have got anything of the Spirit of God in you, your heart goes out to them. You know that it has cost them something. You know that it has meant something to them, and your heart begins to warm towards them. They are not just sitting there like some little dear church member, but they are really moving, seeking to move with God.

May the Lord help us in this matter. I think there is such a need, don't you? Both on the one hand, of this real knowing and experiencing the freedom of our Lord, and on the other hand, really knowing that love of God filling our hearts and lives.

Shall we pray?

Now Lord, oh, we just commit this to Thee. Thou knowest all the areas of need in our lives here, Lord. Thou knowest the area of need in us as a people. Dear Lord, how glad we are that Thou hast spoken to us about doing something. Lord, let it come home to us that there is some responsibility placed on us to loose bonds of wickedness, to undo bands of the yoke, to let the oppressed go free, to break every yoke, to deal our bread to the hungry, to bring the poor that is cast out into our house, and when we see him that is naked, to cover him, and not to hide ourselves from our own flesh. Lord, grant that we may hearken to this. Only Thy Holy Spirit can make it real in each of our circumstances, in each family, each home, in each life and in our life together as a people. Lord, watch over this word and let it really be translated by Thy Spirit into practical outworking. We ask it all in the name of our Lord Jesus.

5.
The Work and the Glory of Zion

Isaiah 60

Arise, shine, for thy light is come and the glory of the Lord is risen upon thee. For, behold darkness shall cover the earth, and gross darkness the peoples; but the Lord will arise upon thee, and His glory shall be seen upon thee. And nations shall come to thy light, and kings to the brightness of thy rising.

Lift up thine eyes round about, and see: they all gather themselves together, they come to thee; thy sons shall come from far, and thy daughters shall be carried in the arms. Then thou shalt see and be radiant, and thy heart shall thrill and be enlarged; because the abundance of the sea shall be turned unto thee, the wealth of the nations shall come unto thee. The multitude of camels shall cover thee, the dromedaries of Midian and Ephah, all they from Sheba shall come; they shall bring gold and frankincense, and shall proclaim the praises of the Lord. All the flocks of Kedar shall be gathered together unto thee, the rams of Nebaioth shall minister unto thee; they shall come up with acceptance on mine altar; and I will glorify the house of my glory. Who are these that fly as a cloud, and as the doves to their windows? Surely the aisles shall wait for me, and the ships of Tarshish first, to bring thy sons from far, their silver, and their gold with them, for the name of the Lord thy God, and for the Holy One of Israel, because he has glorified thee.

And foreigners shall build up thy walls, and their kings shall minister unto thee: for in my wrath I smote thee, but in my favor, have I had mercy on thee. Thy gates shall be open continually; they shall not be shut day nor night; that men may bring onto thee the wealth of the nations, and their kings led captive. For that nation and kingdom that will not serve thee shall perish; yea, those nations shall be utterly wasted. The glory of Lebanon shall come unto thee, the fir-tree, the pine, and the box-tree together, to beautify the place of my sanctuary; and I will make the place of my feet glorious. And the sons of them that afflicted thee shall come bending unto thee; and all they that despised thee shall bow themselves down at the soles of thy feet; and they shall call thee The city of the Lord, The Zion, of the Holy One of Israel.

Whereas thou hast been forsaken and hated, so that no man passed through thee, I will make thee an eternal excellency, a joy of many generations. Thou shalt also suck the milk of the nations and shalt suck the breast of kings; and thou shalt know that I, the Lord, am thy Savior, and Redeemer, the Mighty One of Jacob. For brass I will bring gold and for iron I will bring silver, and for wood brass, and for stones iron. I will also make *thy officers peace, and thine exactors righteousness. Violence shall no more be heard in thy land, desolation nor destruction within the borders; but thou shall call thy walls Salvation, and thy gates Praise. The sun shall no more be thy light by day; neither for brightness shall the moon give light unto thee: but the Lord will be unto thee an everlasting light, and thy God thy glory. Thy sun shall no more go down, neither shall thy moon withdraw itself; for the Lord will be thine everlasting light, and the days of thy mourning shall be ended. Thy people also shall be all righteous; they shall inherit the land for ever, the branch of my planting the work of my hands, that I may be glorified. The little one shall become a thousand, and the small one a strong nation; I, the Lord will hasten it in its time.*

We have been really considering this word, this name, this title: *Zion*. We have been seeking to understand by the Spirit what the Bible really means by the use of this name, because it is not just found in one or two places in the Bible, but it is one of the most common names found in the Scriptures. It runs right the way through even the New Testament. We are told, for instance, by the writer of the Hebrew letter that those who have been born of God, have been saved by the grace of God, "Ye are come unto Mount Zion, unto the city of the living God, unto the heavenly Jerusalem," and so on (Hebrews 12:22). We have been looking at this matter.

We considered the 62nd chapter of Isaiah and those words that command that challenge of the Lord to those who would enter into the fellowship of His travail for Zion. He says, "For Zion's sake, I will not hold my peace, and for Jerusalem's sake I will not rest, until her righteousness go forth as brightness, and her salvation as a lamp that burneth." Then we considered something of that fellowship of His travail into which He would bring us if we really will commit ourselves. The challenge is: "Go through, go through the gates; prepare ye the highway ... for the people. Cast up, cast up the highway; gather out the stones; lift up an ensign for the peoples." We considered some of those ways in which we can prepare the way of the people, in which we are casting up a highway for the people: gathering out the stones, lifting up the ensign, as it were, running the flag up the mast so that everybody can see under whose standard we stand and serve, and whose territory it is we are found within.

Freedom for the Oppressed

We also have considered two things in Isaiah chapter 58. The first was this whole matter of oppression. This is not just a side line, the whole matter of bondage, the whole matter of oppression. We have it in Isaiah 58:6, "Is not this the fast that I have chosen: to loose the bonds of wickedness, to undo the bands of the yoke, and to let the oppressed go free, and that ye break every yoke?" This is not just a deliverance ministry. It is not some particular, specific kind of ministry for those who are rather unusual. Now and again, we find people who are bound or who are oppressed and we have a specific ministry in the body of the Lord Jesus for such ones, but it is not just that. This is dealing with the heart of the matter as far as this world goes.

The Lord Jesus spoke of Satan as the prince of this world. In another place, the apostle Paul, in Ephesians 2, spoke of "the spirit that now worketh in [or energises] the sons of disobedience." He called him "the prince of the power of the air, the spirit that now energises the sons of disobedience." In another place, the Lord Jesus said, speaking of very decent people, "Ye are all of your father, the devil. He was a liar from the beginning" (John 8:44). In other words, fallen mankind has got the poison in its bloodstream and somehow we have been fathered by Satan. We have something of his nature in us. Now that explains human history, doesn't it? We can see six thousand years of bloodshed, strife, disunity, and corruption, while yet there has been a widespread desire for prosperity, peace, unity, equality, and justice. Yet somehow or other each new ideology, each new philosophy, each new political system that is raised up and promises us a golden age, a golden millennia, ends in a bigger dungeon than ever. The ideal may be freedom, equality, and justice but how does it work out unless it is the gospel that comes and liberates men and women? Without the gospel justice becomes injustice, equality becomes inequality, freedom becomes a dungeon and men's joy becomes misery.

Now this is human history. Therefore, the Holy Spirit takes up this matter and says the ministry of Zion, the work of Zion is to proclaim liberty for the captives. In other words, no man or woman can come to know the Lord Jesus Christ, unless God breaks the power of Satan in that person's life. The person may be a very decent person, a very moral person, a very upright person, but they can be blinded by their own self-righteousness so they do not see their need to be born of God. They do not see their need to be saved by the grace of God. You know, that bondage can be as terrible as a bondage to immorality, or a bondage to alcohol, or a bondage to drugs, or a bondage to some other unclean or destructive thing. Only the Lord can break it and He is the one who was anointed by God. That is what His title means: Messiah, or Christ, the Anointed One, anointed by God, to proclaim liberty to those who are captives, the opening of the prison to them that are bound. It is a breaking of every form of captivity so that men and women can come to know Him.

Is it not wonderful that there are many of us who have been delivered from the power of darkness and transferred into the kingdom of His dear Son? That is exactly what the apostle Paul says in Colossians 1:13. It does not matter how decent you were, how religious your background, there came a point when God issued the word and you were delivered from the power of darkness and transferred out of one domain into another, out of one authority into another, out of the powers of darkness into the kingdom of God's dear Son. Wonderful!

Now, I think that this whole matter of loosing bonds of wickedness, undoing the bands of the yoke, letting the oppressed go free, breaking every yoke is absolutely essential. If Zion is to be restored, if Zion is to be completed, if the kingdom of God is to come in power, then we have to tackle this subject because it is the heart of the matter. Isaiah 58:6 speaks of this.

Then in verse seven we spoke of the need, the vital necessity, of love and compassion in all our relationships. Here we have these wonderful words: "Deal thy bread to the hungry, bring the poor that is cast out into thy house, when thou seest the naked, cover him; and that thou hide not thyself from thine own flesh."

In other words, it is no good just getting a vision which is metallic and mechanical. It is no good just having your head filled with doctrine. Unless the Holy Spirit sheds abroad in our hearts the love of God, the compassion of God, and the mercy of God, there is no hope.

In 1 Corinthians, chapter 13 is right in the midst of a whole passage about the body of Christ, the Lord's table, our gathering together unto Him and about how the body of the Lord functions with all its gifts and so on. It goes on about the operation of gifts in chapter 14. Right in the middle of it comes this marvellous chapter on love. He says, "I will show thee the most excellent way" (1 Corinthians 12:31b). Then he says, "You can preach, but if you have not love, it is nothing. You can give your body to be burned, but if you have not love, it means nothing" (1 Corinthians 13). Now if a person gives their body to be burned, you would have thought they had done that out of love, but no. Evidently, you can be martyred for a principle. The Lord says that is no good. The difference between the gospel martyrs and other martyrs is that the other martyrs die for a principle. We die out of love for the Lord and for a world that is lost. God preserve us from just being slaves to doctrine. I am not running down doctrine; it is absolutely essential to have sound doctrine. Truth is of as great importance now as it has ever been in the history of the church. But you know dear friends, whatever we may say, in the end the fact comes back to this: that you can have truth and it can be hard, mechanical, and cold. We can know all the purpose of God and know what He wants and talk endlessly about the church, about being built together and all the rest, even talk about intercession for the nation, yet there are people in our midst who are in desperate need, and we do not share our bread with them. There are people who are destitute and lonely who we do not bring into our homes. The thing has to come right down. We cannot be watchmen on the walls of Zion, we cannot be committed to what the Lord is doing in Zion, unless somehow or other the bread that God has given us is shared, not only physically, naturally, but even the spiritual bread.

I must just say something to the folks here. I know people all over the place who would have given an arm or a leg if they could just live near a company of believers like we have in Halford House, to be able to know the fellowship, to know the ministry, and to be able to share in this. Yet many of us who have been here for years have gotten so blasé about the whole thing. We are so used to it all. What we need to do is share our bread with the hungry. We need to get right down to it. What does it mean? What can we do? What would the Lord have us do? We all have to face the Lord one day and He is going to say to you, "I gave you so much. What did you do about it? Did you hold it to yourself? Did you just become a lot of murmurers, sort of self-contented, with middle-aged spread, well-fed? Did you somehow just say, 'We've got this; we've got that.'"

Oh, if you could only understand the famine that there is amongst the people of God. If you could only know the need that there is amongst the family of God, and the call that comes to us: "Deal thy bread to the hungry. Bring the poor that is cast out into thy house. When you see him that is naked, cover him" (Isaiah 58:7). Don't condemn him, cover him! Oh, when we find someone uncovered, we talk about it: "Have you heard about So-and-So? So-and-So was a servant of the Lord. He has fallen into sin.

Have you heard? He did this and this and this. Dreadful isn't it?" When you see him that is naked and stripped, cover him. Pray for him. Get down beside him. Seek to restore him in a spirit of meekness, considering yourselves, lest you also be tempted.

We need to face some of these things. Everywhere I go I find people with these kinds of problems, people who are in need, and somehow or other those dear ones have been overlooked. We are all so busy that we overlook the people in need: the destitute, the lonely, the afflicted (and I do not just mean people who look as if they are destitute and afflicted and lonely). There are some people who seem to have been really serving the Lord well, but in their heart, they are destitute. They are in great need, but only love and compassion detect such destitution, nothing else. We never see beneath the surface. We never look. We do not go deeper than the skin when it is just a matter of truth. But when there is love and compassion, we see into the heart.

The Yoke in Our Midst

Then, in verses 9–10, the first thing is, "If thou take away from the midst of thee the yoke." Secondly, take away "the putting forth of the finger, and speaking wickedly." Then thirdly, "draw out your soul to the hungry, and satisfy the afflicted soul." Now, this is very interesting because this time the Lord speaks here about the yoke in our midst. Before it was not the yoke in our midst, it was just "loose the bonds of wickedness ... undo the bands of the yoke ... let the oppressed go free and ... break every yoke."

Then it came nearer home: "Deal your bread to the hungry," share your bread with the hungry. "Bring the poor that is cast out into your house. When you see the naked, cover him." You cover him and "hide not yourself from your own flesh". Now, we suddenly find that the Lord is talking about in our midst, in your midst: "If thou take away from the midst of thee the yoke ... the putting forth for the finger, and speaking wickedly, and draw out your soul to the hungry and satisfy the afflicted soul." Now it has come home to ourselves.

Look, dear ones, now we are talking about those within the gates. You know, we are soldiers. Many a time soldiers receive wounds and sometimes our attitude toward one another can be a metallic attitude, a mechanical attitude. We do not understand sometimes these wounds that people receive. Indeed, the terrible nature is that sometimes we leave them to it and we condemn them for it. If we are really in this battle for Zion, there are going to be casualties. What a lovely thing our Lord Jesus said about the twelve, whom God had given Him in John 17:9–10 "I pray for them: I pray not for the world, but for those whom Thou hast given Me: for they are Thine: and all things that are Mine are Thine, and Thine are Mine: and I am glorified in them." Verse 12, "While I was with them, I kept them in Thy name which Thou hast given Me, and I guarded them, and not one of them perished, but the son of perdition."

Now, don't you think that is interesting? Did you hear the words of the Lord Jesus? Does this explain those nights of prayer? Does this explain His prayer life? He said, "Father, You have given me these twelve. I have kept them in Thy name." What does it mean *I kept them in Thy name*? Somehow or other the Lord Jesus saw that in the name of God, in the name of the living God, there was authority. He covered them in the name of the Lord. He kept them in the name of the Lord. He, as it were, guarded them, and not one of them is lost.

Now, I would have thought that we could have said, "Well, what was the need of all that? Surely, if they were chosen by God, and foreordained by God, there was no need for the Lord Jesus to keep them." But listen to me very carefully: anyone who comes into association with the King is at the heart of the battle, and the closer your relationship to the King, and the nearer you get to the heart of the matter, the greater the battle will be.

This is even so of servants of the Lord, if I may just say it as an aside. When we come into association with servants of the Lord, those whom God has really anointed and is using, we come into a battle. All kinds of things begin to happen to us just because of our association with them in the work of the Lord. Now, what are we to do? We need to learn this lesson of keeping the whole family in the name of the Lord, of guarding those whom God has given us that we lose none. Otherwise, as we go along, there will come the inexplicable. Strange things will come in, shafts, fiery darts of the enemy, something suddenly coming in and just waylaying someone; they are knocked out. Before we know where we are, we have this casualty and that casualty and the other casualty.

Will you notice what the Lord tells us to do? He says we are to take away the yoke from our midst. Now I find this interesting. It means that there can be a yoke in the midst of God's people. Here we are, God's liberated, freed people and yet there can be a yoke in our midst. What is this yoke? Well, it can be all kinds of things. It can be undealt with sin, it can be some kind of thing that has been carried over from the past, something of which we have never repented. Sometimes God has to put his finger upon those things. We have to face them and bring it right out into the open and really know what it is to have that yoke broken.

I think what I have mentioned before is very true in this connection. The enemy is all the time seeking to bring a heaviness into the atmosphere, to bring us into some kind of rut, into a routine. Now, everything has to have a routine; I mean, let's face it. I know sometimes we try to keep out of routines, but really and truthfully, in the end, the whole of life is made up of routines of one kind or another. The danger is when the routine becomes a rut when suddenly a kind of *rigour mortis* sets into what we have to do. Then it becomes a straitjacket. Instead of being a vehicle in which the life of God and the way of God is expressed, it becomes a straitjacket in which the way of God and the life of God are limited. We need to watch all this, these yokes.

Don't think for a single moment that the enemy is not trying to bring you back into a yoke. He is. We have to help one another in this manner. This is where there is such a need of openness. If we can open up to one another, we can help one another, especially in our home fellowships. We have a glorious opportunity to really open up to one another, but you know we have one or two problems. First of all, we are all very shy of each other (well, most are). Secondly, we are a little afraid of one another, of what might happen if we let any cats out of the bag. We think" "What will they do? How will they react? What will they do with the information they get?"

You know, some people say, "I'll come and tell *you*, but I'm not going to tell anybody else." This isn't a principle of fellowship. Sometimes we have to say, "I'm sorry, I'm not going to listen," because at times you have got to go to your brothers and sisters because it is not your brothers and sisters, it is the whole principle that is involved. It is the Lord in the midst of His own. If you cannot confess your faults one to another, there is no hope. It means you do not trust your brothers and sisters; you have no confidence in your brothers and sisters. In other words, when it comes down to the final analysis, you do not trust the Lord in them.

There has to come a point where we are really ready to come right down to rock bottom and open up to one another and not be afraid to say, "I feel that somehow a kind of deadness has come into my life or a bondage has come into me in some way. I find myself unable to do this or that. Pray for me." What a wonderful thing it is when we are able to open up like this to one another and really pray for one another in these ways.

What about this, "putting forth of the finger and speaking wickedly"? What is this "putting forth of the finger"? (Isaiah 58:9b). Well, it is just simply this kind of thing. Isn't it amazing how we all know someone who is the problem? Do you know what I mean? Sometimes people can listen to this kind of message and actually be thinking: "I hope So-and-So is getting this." Now, without even realising it, you have been putting forth the finger. It is the most effective psychological way of deflecting God's Word from ourselves. We all do this. Have you ever known someone, who, the moment you start to get near whatever is their problem, immediately begins to talk to you about somebody else? They deflect the whole conversation. The woman of Samaria did that when the Lord was getting a bit too near to the bone in the matter. She suddenly said, "Oh, I perceive that You're a prophet" (John 4:19) and brought up a whole theological problem, but He would have none of it. Do you remember? It was all to do with her husband. In the end, the whole facade fell to pieces and she stood there before him for what she really was and found the Lord.

Now, my point is this: putting forth of the finger is one of the great problems in the fellowship of God's people. What does James say about this matter? He says quite a bit actually. I do not know if you have ever really read this but listen to these words in James 3:1–6: "Be not many of you teachers, my brethren [teachers use the tongue], knowing that we shall receive heavier judgment. For in many things we all stumble. If any stumble not in word, the same is a perfect man, able to bridle the whole body also. Now if we put the horses' bridles into their mouths that they may obey us, we turn about their whole body also. Behold the ships also, though they are so great and are driven by rough winds, are yet turned about by a very small rudder, whither the impulse of the steersman willeth. So the tongue also is a little member, and boasteth great things. Behold, how much wood is kindled by how small a fire! And the tongue is a fire: the world of iniquity among our members is the tongue, which defileth the whole body, and setteth on fire the wheel of nature, and is set on fire by hell."

Those are solemn words. The tongue. I don't suppose there is a person reading this who has not sinned with their tongue. I certainly have. Would you not be ready to admit that when you read words like this you know very well that your tongue has led you into real problems, real difficulties? Often, it is a root of bitterness, deep, deep down in our lives, and oh, it comes out. We speak things about another person behind their back. We point the finger at them. We condemn them.

I would love to give some examples of this, but I am afraid that it may not be wise. I have seen some terrible things amongst the people of God. Servants of the Lord, crucified by wicked, wicked tongues. This is why there are some works, some so-called Christian works, that never recover from generation to generation. You can go to certain places which have a history of trouble going back a hundred years because that membership, that community has never repented of things that were said in the presence of the Lord. We may forget the words of our mouths, but they are recorded. As the Word says, "By every word that you have spoken, you shall be judged" (Matthew 12:36). Now, the only way to get rid of that is to come face to face with it and allow the Lord to deal with it. I say that the tongue is the hardest member in our whole being to really be brought under the government of God.

There is a lot here that speaks about this matter. Look at Galatians 5:14–15, "For the whole law is fulfilled in one word, even in this 'Thou shalt love thy neighbour as thyself.' But if you bite and devour one another, take heed that ye be not consumed one of another." In other words, once we start this pointing of the finger and speaking wickedly about one another, we bite and devour one another, and we are consumed by one another. May the Lord preserve us from such a thing.

Our Lord said in the Gospel of Luke 6:37–38, "Judge not and ye shall not be judged, condemn not, and ye shall not be condemned, release, and ye shall be released, give and it shall be given unto you. Good measure, pressed down, shaken together, running over, shall they give into your bosom."

How would you like to be dealt with? Now, I do not believe, as some believe, in that kind of naive gullibility that you swallow anything about any believer, that you must believe every single word they said. That is not true. The Scripture gives the balance to this: "He that is spiritual judgeth all things" (1 Corinthians 2:15). The difference is this: criticism and spiritual mature judgment are two very different things. You know, just malicious criticism. The way we tear one another to pieces, the way we strip one another, as it were, naked, the way we condemn, and when we point the finger at one another, that is destructive. However, to know where a person stands, to know their failings, to know their faults, and be able to take it to God and love them even the more, that is really maturity.

Do you notice that we are to *take away the putting forth of the finger and speaking wickedly*? Some people don't like this. It is an interesting thing that people who speak very, very wickedly with the tongue, when finally faced with authority on this matter, get terribly upset and go around telling everybody how "the brothers dealt harshly with me, how wickedly they dealt with me." It is a very strange thing that our own worst fault is often what we feel someone else is doing to us. Now, the Word is quite clear here. God does not say, "I will take away the putting forth of the finger," although He does in the end. What He says is that *we* must deal with it.

Now dear friends, don't try and get the mote out of somebody else's eye. Start with the log in your own. If we are going to get rid of this "putting forth of the finger" and this "speaking wickedly" let each one of us repent before the Lord in this matter. Say, "Lord, I don't want to destroy Zion. I don't want to become the means by which the whole work of Zion, the building of Zion is paralysed; I don't want to! Root this thing out of me. Deal with it, Lord. Fill me with love. Somehow or other, bring this tongue of mine under the government of God."

Then you will notice that we are to "draw out our souls to the hungry and satisfy the afflicted" (Isaiah 58:10). That is interesting, isn't it? Drawing out our souls. You see, we at times tend to think that we all know that there are people in need, but we leave it to everybody else. But it says draw out your *soul* to the hungry. You have got to do something. This work of Zion means that you and I have got to care for one another.

Sometimes something happens whereby those within Zion become hungry, poor, destitute, and afflicted. We have got to care for them. If we do not have compassion upon one another, what hope is there? If love does not start with the household of God, what hope is there? We can talk about longing that the Lord would send an awakening to the Thames Valley—and I believe that in the end, something will happen for we have had enough promises over the last 25 years on this matter. However, I sometimes wonder whether the Lord has to hold up because He is saying, "My people are just not ready. If I were to bring something where thousands upon thousands were swept into the kingdom, what would happen? The weaknesses that have not been dealt with would just come right out and break up the whole thing." So, we have to face these things. Where there are problems amongst us and in us, let God really deal with them.

The Promise

What a wonderful promise we have as a result of this. If we will take away this yoke from the midst of us, the putting forth of the finger and speaking wickedly, and if we will draw out our soul to the hungry and satisfy the afflicted soul, then comes the promise:

"Thy light shall rise in darkness" (Isaiah 58:10). There may be thick darkness everywhere, but God says, "My dawn will dawn on you. A new day will begin with you in your area amongst that people in that nation and thine gloom, thine obscurity should become as noonday, thy gloom shall be as mid-day."

Then He says, "And the Lord will guide thee continually" (verse 11). What a wonderful word! He says, "I will keep my eye upon them specially. I know their frailty and weakness, but I will guide them continually so there is no chance of them coming out of my will or getting out of my way. I will satisfy their soul in scorched places. I will make strong their bones. [That is, the inner part of them which gives rise to all their healthiness.] I will look after that; I will make it My responsibility." What a promise! If we will only deal with these things, God says, "I will take care of the heart of the whole work. I will look after the bones and the marrow. I will see that the bones are strong. I will see that they are guided continually in the centre of My will."

Then He goes on and says, "They shall be like a spring of water whose waters fail not, a watered garden." Well, that is lovely. (We here, of course, have plenty of water and you have certainly had enough rain I understand in the last few months.) But oh, how wonderful it is in countries which are dry and hot and arid to walk into a garden. It is just like reviving. Sometimes, when one goes round Jerusalem on various errands or doing various things and walks into the garden tomb area, your spirit revives as you step in—all that greenery, all those trees—it just does something to you. In a hot country, a garden means something. What a wonderful promise then that we shall "be like a watered garden, and like a spring of water, whose waters fail not. And they that shall be of thee shall build the old waste places; they shalt raise up the foundations of many generations; and thou shalt be called the repairer of the breach, the restorer of streets in which to dwell" (verses 11–12).

The Rights of the Lord

Now look at this last thing that the Lord speaks about that I would call: *the rights of the Lord.* "If thou turn away thy foot from the sabbath, from doing thy pleasure on my holy day; and call the sabbath a delight, *and* the holy of the Lord honourable; and shalt honour it, not doing thine own ways, nor finding thine own pleasure, nor speaking *thine own* words: then shalt thou delight thyself in the Lord; and I will make thee to ride upon the high places of the earth; and I will feed thee with the heritage of Jacob thy father: for the mouth of the Lord hath spoken it" (verses 13–14).

What is the Sabbath? Now, I know that there may be some who come from a background where they belong to that very strict Sabbatarianism—Sunday is the Sabbath and all the law that we have in the Old Testament is applied to that day. Well, the Lord bless you. As the Scripture says, if there are those who keep Sabbaths, let them keep them. If they feel they should keep it unto the Lord, let them keep it unto the Lord, but what I want to talk about is the principle of the Sabbath keeping.

Why did the Lord take one day in seven and say, "You must give this one day to Me"? Now straightaway, of course, there is the whole question of health. There is no doubt about it, that one day of recreation, of rest, of doing something different than the other six days has a very real effect upon us mentally and physically. However, I think it is dangerous when we think of it like that, because then when people think of Sunday they think, "Well, what's the point of coming together in meetings? Why don't we go out to the park? Why not go down to the swimming pool and have a swim? That is recreation and rest. I don't get any mental refreshment from that lot, sitting with them in that hot room. I think it would be better to go ..."

Do you see that kind of an argument? That is not the Sabbath. It may be one of the by-products of the Sabbath, but the main point of the Sabbath is the rights of the Lord. It is as if He is saying, "Now remember, this day is My day and on this day, you remember that you are Mine, that I have redeemed you that you belong to Me and the other six days are to be lived in the light of the Sabbath." The rights of the Lord. You see He says, "... if you will only turn away thy foot from the Sabbath, from doing thy pleasure on My holy day; and call the Sabbath a delight, and holy unto the Lord, [holy unto the Lord, separated unto the Lord], you shall call it a delight" (verse 13).

Many people do not find the rights of the Lord a delight. They find it almost a bondage. This is a mental conception. I say this without fear of contradiction. In all the years that I have belonged to the Lord and the years I have been in His ministry, I have never met a person who has given the Lord His rights, who has been bound. Never! I have met a lot of people who say they have given the Lord His rights, yet are in absolute straitjackets. They are serving a doctrine or a movement or a thing. I do not know anybody who has given the Lord His rights, who is not a person who has joy. Do you really think that you can put the Lord in your debt? Never! You think you say, "Lord, I'm going to give

You Your rights. I'm going to be terribly miserable about it, but I'm going to give you your rights. When I've given You Your rights, and I'm terribly miserable about it, just You remember, I gave You Your rights."

You know, this is the kind of mentality we have with the Lord. We sort of say, "Lord, You know, You're in my debt. You're in my debt, Lord. I've had to sacrifice this for You and that for You and the other for You; and I didn't do this, and I didn't do that, Lord. For *You*, Lord! Just remember, You're in debt, Lord, to me. My life's been quite miserable because of You. A whole lot of things I could have done if I had just not been thinking about You. Yet because of You I've had to do this and this and this. Now, just You remember, Lord You're in my debt." The Lord is no man's debtor!

All These Things Shall Be Added

If you give the Lord His right, He will fill you in the end with such joy, such peace and such fullness that you will forever praise Him for what He is. You will never be talking about, "Lord, just you remember what I've done for you;" you will never think of it. You will just find it a privilege to serve Him and a privilege to know Him. These are the people who really have given the Lord His rights.

What does it mean? Put first things first; that is what it means. You have it in Matthew 6:33, "But seek ye first His kingdom, and His righteousness, and all these things shall be added unto you." Did you hear that? What are all these things? What to eat, what to be clothed with, where to sleep, and all these other things.

Did you hear what the Lord said? If you give Him His rights, put first things first, and all these things will be added unto you.

Have you got any problems about these things? Life consists of worrying about these things--where to get the money to buy food, where to get the money to buy clothing, how to pay the rates, how to pay the rent—but you see what the Lord says. He says that if you put first Him and His Kingdom, all these things will be added unto you. It is as if the Lord says, "I'm going to take responsibility for you. You are putting first things first. You've turned away your foot from your own pleasure on My Sabbath. You've called it a delight. You've called it honourable and holy to the Lord. Because you've given Me My rights, because you've put first things first, I will come into your life and do for you far more than you could have ever believed possible." Oh, the Lord will do this, for one after another of us, if we would only take this step of giving Him His rights.

See what the Lord says here in this same chapter, in Matthew 6:21–24. "For where thy treasure is, there will thy heart be also. The lamp of the body is the eye: if therefore thine eye be single, thy whole body shall be full of light. But if thine eye be evil, thy whole body shall be full of darkness. If therefore the light that is in thee be darkness, how great is the darkness! No man can serve two masters: for either he will hate the one, and love the other; or else he will hold to one, and despise the other. Ye cannot serve God and mammon."

I think because of the Old English, we think of an evil eye as being an eye for pornography. You know, it is a kind of eye that picks up the wrong things. Now, I am quite sure that is true. I think an evil eye will lead to your whole body being full of darkness, but what our Lord really meant by evil eye is double vision. If you get anything wrong with your eyes, and you do not have focused vision, you can get into real trouble. For starters, you can get very bad headaches. Another thing is that you just do not see. Any of you who have got problems with your eyes, you know this don't you? One eye sees more clearly and the other eye does not so the two have a little battle. Believe me, your whole body is full of darkness. Some of you know what it is to get really severe headaches because there is something wrong with vision as we get older. It is a wonderful thing to have properly harmonised vision and to see things clearly. My point is this: our Lord said, if there is something wrong with your sight, with your eyes, if you are seeing two things all the time, your whole body will be full of darkness. On the contrary, if you have a single eye, that is, both eyes are focused, and your whole body will be full of light.

Now, come back to this Isaiah 58. What does he say? He says, "Then shalt thou delight thyself in the Lord" (verse 14). Oh, what a wonderful word! When we give the Lord His rights, it is as if the Lord unveils His heart to us. Some people come to me and say, "You know, I sought the Lord and He never met me." Well, maybe it is something to do with this kind of thing. We have got to give the Lord His rights and come under His lordship. When we do that, when we come to that place, then it says, "Then shalt thou delight thyself in the Lord, and I will make thee to ride upon the high places of the earth and I will feed thee with the heritage of Jacob thy father."

What is the heritage of Jacob thy father? Grace, more grace, and more grace, and even more grace! That is the heritage of Jacob your father. The Lord fed him with grace. He lived by grace.

He was transformed by grace. He fulfilled the purpose of God through the grace of God. It was grace from beginning to end. He fed on the faithfulness of the Lord. So it will be with you.

What about riding "upon the high places of the earth"? This means you shall not be beneath, but above. You shall not be the tail, but you will be the head. Praise the Lord, what a promise! If I give the Lord His rights, the enemy will certainly try to squash me, but it does not matter. The Lord will bring me out on top every time because He has promised, "I will cause thee to ride upon the high places of the earth" (verse 14). It is the principle of the cross: you go down, but you go up. If you go down, you will certainly go up. The farther down you go, the farther up you will go. Is that not wonderful? "I will cause thee to ride upon the high places of the earth."

… and the Glory of the Lord Is Risen upon Thee

Well, we must bring all this to a close. You see what a wonderful thing the whole matter is! We read these wonderful words in Isaiah 60:1–2 which we read a little earlier, "Arise, shine, for thy light is come, and the glory of the Lord is risen upon thee. For behold, darkness shall cover the earth and gross darkness the peoples, but the Lord will arise upon thee, and His glory shall be seen upon thee."

Isn't it interesting that one or two of these promises are just about this? It says in Isaiah 58:8, "Then shall thy light break forth as the morning, and thy healing shall spring forth speedily." Or again in verse 10, "Then shall thy light rise in darkness, and thy gloom be as mid-day." Listen: "Arise, shine for thy light has come, and the glory of the Lord is risen upon thee." Do not think that is just going to be easy. It says that darkness will cover the earth, and gross darkness the peoples, but the Lord will arise upon thee and His glory shall be seen upon thee.

Dear friends, I am perfectly prepared for gross darkness if it means that the glory of the Lord is seen upon her, the Zion of God. Then the very darkness of the nations, the very darkness of the whole political systems of this world, will only drive men and women, who want truth and long for God, into the light. It will be like a beacon that will flash out over a vast, vast area so that people can see it and turn to the Lord.

What does the Lord say here? Listen to these wonderful words in the last part of Isaiah 60:7 "I will glorify the house of My glory," and the last part of verse nine, "the Holy One of Israel because He hath glorified thee." Or again, the last part of verse 13, "I will make the place of My feet glorious," or the last part of this, "and they shall call thee the city of the Lord, the Zion of the Holy One of Israel" (verse 14).

Dear people of God, what a wonderful thing it is to know this glory of the Lord upon us. In the New Testament, in II Corinthians 3:18b it says that we are taken on from glory to glory. This, of course, does not just mean from ecstasy to ecstasy. It means from one capacity of glory to another capacity of glory, but how wonderful the Lord is to us that He does touch us at times with His glory, doesn't He? It is not all just sort-of having to battle through and go on and on. There are times when the glory of the Lord touches us, when we know that the Lord is manifesting Himself, when we know that somehow or other those invisible forces are witnessing the power of God and a demonstration of the Lord, the Holy Spirit—Zion.

In Isaiah 12:6 it says, "Cry aloud and shout, thou inhabitants of Zion; for great in the midst of thee is the Holy One of Israel." I don't know what these times have meant to many of you, but there is one thing about which I think we can be absolutely certain. This whole question of Zion is of the utmost importance to the Lord.

Coming back to Psalm 2:6–8: "Yet have I set my king upon Zion, the mountain of my holiness, I will tell the decree, the Lord said unto me, thou art my Son, this day have I begotten thee. Ask of me, and I will give thee the nations for thine inheritance, and the uttermost parts of the earth, for thy possession."

The Lord purposes glory for His people. I wish that we could all rise up as one to really pray that somehow the glory of the Lord might not only touch us, but through us touch the community here in which we live, and the Thames Valley, and this whole nation. Do you believe it is possible? I say, it is absolutely possible. Every single time that the Spirit of God has really worked in the history of the Church, He started with some insignificant man, some little, tiny group of people, and through them He has turned the world upside down. Look what He did in Jerusalem right at the beginning: 120 unknowns, and with them He turned Jerusalem upside down, and then Judea, and then Samaria, and then to the uttermost parts of the earth.

God has not changed. He can do the whole thing again, if once the King is in His place in Zion, if once Zion is being built, if once the purpose of the Lord is seen, if once there is a taking, as it were, of the nations for the Lord, this exercising of dominion over the principalities and powers, over the nations—three things: the King, Zion, and the uttermost parts of the earth for His possession.

I quoted this earlier from Numbers 14:21: "As truly as I live, saith the Lord, the earth shall be filled with the glory of God." The prophet Isaiah said in Isaiah 11:9: "For the earth shall be full of the knowledge of the Lord, as the waters cover the sea." Habakkuk put it this way: "And the earth shall be full of the knowledge of the glory of the Lord, as the waters cover the sea" (Habakkuk 2:14).

The Lord has tremendous purposes of glory. Think for a moment about this dear old creation around us, which we are so destroying, and polluting and damaging. Do you really believe that this wonderful creation, which has existed for so many thousands of years, is what God originally intended? No, I do not, myself. We see within it, as it were, something of the original design, something of the original purpose, and the more we see what there is in this natural creation, the more it fills our hearts with worship and praise. It is so wonderful, such a harmony, such a fine balance. It is incredible! Yet we understand that it has never fulfilled the original purpose of God, as it says in Romans 8:20–21: "For the creation was subjected to vanity, not of his own will, but by reason of Him who subjected it in hope that the creation itself also shall be delivered from the bondage of corruption into the liberty of the glory of the children of God."

Now, this thrills me, because it means that every tree, every flower, every animal, is only a shadow of the original idea. It is as if somehow or other, we just see something that is the faintest, faintest, faintest idea of what God originally wanted.

However, man, the heart of the whole thing fell; and because man fell, it was as if the hub fell out of the whole wheel. The centre was destroyed and the whole thing was subjected to vanity, not because the creation itself was evil, but because man fell. Therefore, God subjected it to vanity, an endless cycle of seasons, out of which it can never, never, never burst forth.

God has a purpose for this earth. The apostle Peter put it very simply in Acts 3:20–21 that He must send the Messiah "… who has been appointed for you, even Jesus, whom the heaven must receive, until the times of restoration of all things, whereof God spake by the mouth of His holy prophets that have been from of old." There is a time coming, when everything is going to be restored.

When we come to the last chapters of the Bible, what do we find? We find the King, and we find His Zion, and we hear these wonderful words, "Behold, I make all things new. The former things have passed away, behold, I make all things new." What are the former things? Sorrow, death, crying, pain, these things belong to the former world. It has passed away. "He that sitteth on the throne," it says, "maketh all things new" (Revelation 21:5). Oh, I want to be in that; I want to be in that!

Listen, young person. You may not even know why you are a Christian. You may not even know why God has saved you. Do you know that the grace of God is so wonderful toward you, young ones, that God has saved you and brought you into an invincible movement for the liberation of the world? This is a movement. You know the communists speak of the inexorable march of history, the onward march of history. They say it is inexorable, what is going to happen is going to happen. It is all part of the evolutionary process. Well, let them think that. All I know is this: I do not think there is ever any evolutionary process like that. I believe God is behind the evolution if there is one. To me, the wonderful thing is this: there is a movement that began in heaven and came with the Redeemer to bring back, not just man to Himself, but the whole universe to Himself. So that in the end, the original purpose of God for this dear old earth will be fulfilled. I want to be part of that. Every time I see this earth polluted, every time I see what fallen man has done to this poor old world, I weep inside. Then I think: There is coming a day when the King will come and when the King will come, it will not be a day of politics anymore. It will not be a day of diplomacy anymore. He will not have to shake hands with evil murderers, and sort-of try to plan some coexistence with them. He will not have to have them to the table to talk with them and try to work out some way of keeping everything in balance. Thank God, righteousness will be the foundation of His throne, and what is truth will be said and done and obeyed! Oh, what a day!

People say to me, "Well, you must be an absolute, wild fanatic. Fancy believing something like that! Do you really believe that?" I do believe it. I absolutely do. I am a Messianist. I cannot be anything else. Every other thing in this world has failed, has it not? Every single system—socialist, capitalist, or whatever else— it has all failed. There is only one hope for this world. It will never grow better and better and better until the golden age.

I have lived long enough to hear Churchill and others tell us, "... the golden age is just around the corner. We are marching into the golden era." We have never marched into it. My goodness me, we have never marched into the golden era. I love Mr. Churchill.

I think God raised him up at the right time as far as this country and the Free World were concerned, but my goodness me, we never marched into that golden era, that golden age. We never will. It will not come by just a process. It will come by divine intervention. Suddenly, one day there will appear in the heavens the sign of the Son of Man.

I don't know what the sign is, but it will be in the heavens. When that sign comes, He will come with great power and glory in the clouds of heaven. I believe it with all my heart. There is no other hope for this world. Man in his present state just has to coexist with evil, he has to somehow just try to keep the whole thing in check. Everything starts out as if it has got great hope and ends in failure and catastrophe, but when this Messiah comes, then at last peace will come to the earth and righteousness and unity. Death will be banished and sorrow, and sighing, and pain, and anguish; all those things will have passed away. They belong to the former things. Then, friends, oh the thrill of it!

People say to me, "I think heaven is going to be so boring." Now be honest, some of you youngsters, you have said it to me at times. You dare not tell some of the others, but you have said it to me. You have said to me when you opened your heart, "I think heaven will be dreadfully boring. Is it going to be like those endless meetings where we just sing and sing and sing and sing?"

It seems that some people give us the idea that in heaven we can have great worship time for a thousand years. Then, after we have had a thousand years' worship time, we will have a little sort of interlude where the angels will serve tea or coffee according to your like. Then, after an interlude of 500 years, a bell will ring and we will have a two thousand year time of worship. After that, another bell will ring and we will have another little interlude where we will sort-of sit around in heaven on our golden thrones. Afterwards, there will be another long great session!

It is nothing like that at all. Not at all. No one knows what is stored up for the ages to come. It is a secret. We only have a glimpse that it is connected with the liberty of the glory of the children of God. When God has got His Zion, when God has got that bride without spot, without blemish so that she can be presented to Him, when He has brought her to the place where she can be the queen, where she can reign with Him jointly from the throne, then this whole chapter that we have all known in time will be over. The glorious chapters that are yet to be written, will be written one by one. We shall see these trees developing into whatever God meant them to be. Is that not amazing? That is why the prophet says the trees will clap their hands. He says the hills will shout for joy.

I want to be in that. I do not find that the least bit boring. When I look at this old world, with all the wonder that is in this universe, I think: "If this is a fallen universe, paralysed and in bondage to corruption and vanity, what is it going to be like in the end, when the whole thing is released?" It is going to be just one word: glory. I want to be part of that, don't you? It is one thing to be saved. It is another thing to be committed to God's Zion and to allow Him not only to bring you into union with Himself and build you together with others locally but to bring you to the place where you learn to reign with Him. That is what it is all about. If the Lord can achieve that for you and for me, praise God!

You know, at the beginning of the age the apostle Paul said some things like this in Romans 8, about the whole creation being on tiptoe, waiting for this thing to happen, waiting for the children of God. If he wrote about that nearly 2000 years ago, people have had to wait a long time. But I can tell you quite confidently, I don't believe we have got that long to wait. We really are in the end. I believe that most of the folks who are here now, your eyes will see the coming of the Messiah because some of the great milestones of prophecy actually have been put in their place. They have been unveiled so that for the first time we know where we are. Praise God! If we are so near to that coming of the Lord, the most obvious thing to do is to go through the gates, to commit oneself, to start this preparing of the way for the people, to cast up the highway, to gather out the stones. God help us. Thine eyes shall see the king in his beauty. Thou shalt see a land of far distances.

Shall we pray?

Dear Lord, we pray together that in Thy mercy and in Thy grace, Thou wilt unveil something of this to our hearts. We want to be in this movement of Thy Spirit. We want to be part of that tremendous movement toward the restoration of all things to Thyself. And we want it to begin with ourselves. We want all rebellion in our hearts to be rooted out, Lord. We want to know the lordship of the King, of the Lord Jesus. We want to know His love shed abroad in our hearts in reality and truth. Lord, only Thou canst deal with us and only Thou canst apply this word to every heart as it ought to be. This we ask in the name of our Lord Jesus. Amen.

6.
Going Through the Gates

Isaiah 62:6–12

I have set watchmen upon my walls, Oh Jerusalem and they shall never hold their peace day nor night. Ye that are the Lord's remembrancers take ye no rest, and give Him no rest, till He establish, and till He make Jerusalem a praise in the earth. The Lord hath sworn by His right hand and by the arm of His strength, surely I will no more give thy grain to be food for thy enemies, and foreigners shall not drink thy new wine for which thou has laboured, but they that have garnered it shall eat it, and praise the Lord, and they that have gathered it shall drink it in the courts of My sanctuary. Go through, go through the gates prepare ye the way of the people, cast up, cast up the highway, gather out the stones, lift up an ensign for the peoples. Behold the Lord hath proclaimed unto the end of the earth, Say ye to the daughter of Zion, Behold, thy salvation cometh, behold, His reward is with Him and His recompense before Him. And they shall call them the holy

I would like to say one final word about the matter that we have been considering. You will remember we have thought very much about Zion. We talked about the battle for Zion, about the building up of Zion, about the travail for Zion, and about the work of Zion or the ministry of Zion. We now look at this 62nd chapter of Isaiah and we hear the words of the Lord Jesus, of the Messiah, in the first verse: "For Zion's sake, will I not hold My peace, and for Jerusalem's sake, I will not rest until her righteousness go forth as brightness, and her salvation as a lamp that burneth." Now, this is not only the literal Zion, and the literal Jerusalem, the literal Israel of this earth. It is perfectly true that this is a very real and deep burden upon the heart of the Messiah at the present time. He will not rest until something happens with that nation, and with that land, and with that city, in preparation for His return.

However, there is this other side that we have been considering which is the Zion which is above. We read of that Zion in Hebrews 12:22: "But ye," that is the redeemed of the Lord, "are come unto Mount Zion, and unto the city of the living God, the Heavenly Jerusalem." We have come, we are seeking that city which has the foundations whose builder and architect is God. We have here no abiding city, but we seek for that which is to come.

Of course, the glorious thing, as it says in Galatians 4:26, is that every single one who is born of God is born in Zion.

God does not disregard the fact that you were born in London, or Tokyo, or Hong Kong, or Singapore, or Orlando, or all these cities and towns from which we come. God does not disregard that. In fact, I want to say something about that in just a moment, but what He does see as the supreme value is whether you have been born in Zion. Now, if you have been born of that Jerusalem which is above, which is free, then Psalm 87 becomes a reality. When He counts up the nations, He will say this one was born there, and that one was born there. They are not born in Ethiopia, or Egypt (Rahab), or in the Sudan, or in Tyre, or in Philistia; they were born in Zion. Your birth is registered, registered in the Lamb's book of life. Beside every single registration in that book is the birthplace: Zion. So, every real believer is a Zionist.

There is not a real believer that is not a Zionist, because we belong to a movement for the liberation of the world. We belong to that movement which is going to end and result in the earth coming back to its rightful owner, the nations becoming the inheritance of the Lord, and the uttermost parts of the earth, His possession. Now, isn't that glorious? That gives us a goal to work for, it gives us an aim, and it gives us a horizon. We are not just saved and left to ourselves wandering around in a circle.

I cannot help feeling so often with some believers, that they seem to be on the 40 years' wilderness wandering. Round and round and round and round they go. They do not really know where they are going. They know that they are out of Egypt, but they do not know where they are going. They just go. They have got experience. They have seen the pillar of cloud and fire by day and by night. They have fed on the manna day by day and they have had water out of the rock. They even know something about the tabernacle, but not too much. I mean, for them, the tabernacle is something that is just there and the glory of the Lord is there. It is wonderful when the Lord speaks there, and there we can offer our offerings and make our sacrifices, but they do not know that the Lord's plan is not for a tabernacle wandering round in the wilderness. His plan is for a Jerusalem which is solid and eternal. His whole plan was that when you come into the promised land, you shall not offer your sacrifices, your offerings where you shall choose on any high place, like the nations which I will drive out before you, but you shall come to the place where I will cause my name to dwell. There you shall offer your offerings and make your sacrifices. That place was Jerusalem.

You know, sometimes we believers have got our experiences of the Lord, and we have blessed experiences of the Lord. We know what it is for Him to provide. We know what it is for Him to lead. We know what it is for Him, as it were, to meet with us. Yet, we are still going on an endless cycle round and round and round the wilderness, as if that is all that matters. As if all that matters is to see the pillar of cloud and fire, to drink the water out of the rock, and to eat bread, the manna that God has provided, and sometimes for the change of diet, to eat quails. I mean, it seems as if that is all that really matters. When the earth opens up and swallows up those who are troublemakers, that is another experience. But that is not the purpose of the Lord. The purpose of the Lord is to get us through the wilderness, to give us experiences of the Lord, but to get us into the land, and into that tremendous purpose of His. It is all bound up with that Zion, all bound up with that Jerusalem. Until the Lord has His King, in His holy hill of Zion, there is no possibility of the nations becoming His inheritance, and the uttermost parts of the earth becoming again His possession.

The Restitution of All Things

The restitution of all things, the restoration of all things is dependent upon the King being in His place in Zion. Secondly, it is dependent upon Zion being built and thirdly, upon Zion fulfilling its ministry. When the King is in His place, and Zion is being built up, and the ministry and work of Zion is being fulfilled, then, and only then do we become truly involved and instrumental in the ends of the earth coming back to their rightful owner and the nations being brought, as it were, under the government of our Lord.

The wonderful thing about this whole matter is that God has got His King in Zion. There is no question about it. It says in Psalm 2:6, "Yet have I set my King upon my holy hill of Zion." He has done it! There is no question about it. There is no question of the Lord Jesus being dethroned or unseated. There is no question of the purpose of God concerning the Lord Jesus being frustrated. God has set Him in His Zion. He is there at the right hand of God the Father, and He has sat down until the Father makes all His enemies the footstool of His feet. So, the word goes out in Psalm 110:2 "The Lord will send forth the rod of thy strength out of Zion. Rule Thou in the midst of Thine enemies." It is said of the Lord Jesus.

Now, how can He do that if all we have is a Zion which is in the "Never Never"? How can we do that if our Zion, if our Jerusalem is so above that we never see it, if the only relationship we have with it is a very tenuous relationship, something to do with our conversion and that is the only relationship we have with Zion? No, dear friends, where is this Zion built? I want to say this straightaway: this Zion is built down here. It is no good us being butterflies, flitting from one company of believers to another, tasting the ministry here and the ministry there, or going off on this or going off on that. Unless God brings us into the discipline of a local company, community of believers on the right foundation of the Lord Jesus Christ, how is it possible for Zion to be built? We are just living in a fool's paradise, singing songs of Zion, singing wonderful hymns about the glory of the Lord, and the coming Kingdom of the Lord, when we ourselves have nothing to do with it in practice.

All through Church history the Lord has had successive stages which He has completed by the work of the Holy Spirit. In the last part of this age, there are a final few stages to be completed, to be, as it were, taken or journeyed through. I am not saying that we are going to have novel things. May God preserve us from that. That is one of the dangers at the present time. Because we know we are at the end of the age, people are looking around for novel things that are not even in the Word of God, or cooking up things that are not in the Word of God, but they say are in the Word of God. Thus they are deceiving the people of God. We do not want any of that. What we want to know is the work of our Lord in such fullness, such power, and such reality that we become involved in this whole work of His in the restitution of all things. Praise God for that! That means that it is no good for us just simply to say, "Oh, well, I don't know. I don't find it very interesting. I think I'll go here, or I'll go there, or I'll flit off here, or flit off there." What is the point of that?

There may well come a day when you won't have ministry anyway, where we shall have to go into caves or into sheds or into our homes and meet in twos and threes. What are you going to do then, when all you have spoken about is "wonderful ministry, wonderful ministry, wonderful ministry," and you have despised anything that seems to be rather humdrum and routine? If you have despised just getting to know one another, getting close to one another, praying for one another, and really helping one another through, what is going to happen when those days of persecution finally come and we will not be able to meet together?

Young people, listen to me. The older people may go to be with the Lord; I do not know how long we have. But you younger ones, unless God can do something in us now to really prepare us, what will we do? Unless the Holy Spirit has brought such a flexibility into us that He can, as it were, enable us to meet in the simplest manner to help one another, to pray for one another, to minister to one another, to glorify the Lord together without all the great paraphernalia, what will we do?

Now, I am not against big meetings. We can go too far the other way. We can sort-of have "a thing" about getting together for a good Bible study or a good time of ministry or whatever else and that is just as silly, but you see, this Zion has got to be built here where we are. I do not have much to do with the Zion which is above and the Zion which is to come, if I have not allowed the Lord to do something in my own heart and life here. If I have not learned something of the battle for Zion down here, and known something of the victories and triumphs of the Lord in it, through His finished work. What is the point of talking about the battle of Zion, if we only *talk* about Zion being built up? We sing, "We're marching to Zion, beautiful, beautiful Zion," and of those "fields that yield a thousand sacred sweets." (I always imagine a sweet shop, some sort of booth in the corner of a field sort-of distributing sweets. It is rather wrong, but I'm afraid I cannot get this mental picture out of my head every time we sing that verse.) We sing these wonderful hymns, but what do they mean? They do not mean anything to us. The only thing we are ever used to is sitting in rows listening because we have never come to the place where we really know a building up of Zion inside of us and amongst us so that we are brought together in the Lord. Now this Zion has got to be built *here*. I can talk about the building up of Zion, about the glory of Zion, about His foundation being in Zion, and "glorious things are spoken of Thee, O Zion, city of God," yet really, the whole thing is just in my head (Psalm 87:3).

Where is this Zion built? It is built here. Where is it built? It is built in the locality in which I live. How is it built? It is built in the community of believers of the redeemed who meet very simply in the Lord Jesus Christ with none of these restrictions and labels that divide but simply as believers so that we can really be built up together and flow together with the Lord. It is where the Spirit of the Lord can lead us and do His job.

If the burden of our Lord's heart is for Zion, for its building up and for its completion, am I to believe that all He does is pray? Is it not true that the Holy Spirit actually realises the travail and intercessory ministry of our Lord upon earth? That as the Lord Jesus prays, the Holy Spirit actually performs the things and does the things that He asks for? It must be so. Therefore dear ones, you and I, we want to be in this work of the Lord, do we not? I do not want to talk about Zion all day long every day and sing these lovely hymns, and at the end of it find that I have precious little to do with Zion. I do not want our Lord to say to me, "You know, you were born in Zion, but that's all. Nothing else ever happened because you did not let it happen."

What does it mean then when this word of command comes, "Go through, go through the gates"? (Isaiah 62:10). I have spoken on this once or twice, and I almost hesitate. Every time I think, "Oh dear, they'll all clam up, shut up, and switch off. He will now say, 'Go through, go through' again." But the fact of the matter is, maybe the Lord *is* saying this for the third time: Go through. Go through the gates. What does it mean? Well, as I said last time, it means you have got to commit yourself, not to people firstly, but to the Lord as the King in Zion. That is the first thing. You have got to go through the gates into Zion and be part of what God is doing with Zion. Then you can go through the gates, as it were, out of the gates to build the highway for the people who are to come.

Now, one day it will happen here in this Thames Valley area. I am convinced of it. Whether it is only in the last few years of the age, I do not know. Yet I know in my bones that in the end, the Thames Valley will see an awakening such as it has not seen before. All those early battles that we fought over the Thames Valley and this area, which the Lord again and again said, "I'm going to do this thing; I'm going to do this thing," in the end He will do it. Are we ready for it? If the Lord began to work in such a way that thousands were really saved, swept into the kingdom of God, into the family of God, what would we do? We have enough problems now. As I have often said, there is a problem for every believer. If we have got 250 problems now, when those thousands get saved, we are going to have a few thousand more problems. Now you know as well as I do, thank the Lord, He is the one who is responsible for all these problems, but I am a problem to Him and you are as well. I do not know if you recognise that yet, but we are all problems to the Lord, but my goodness, He knows how to deal with us. Sometimes it takes him 30 or 40 years, but He finally gets His way.

True, Personal Knowledge of the King

Now, all I want to say is what it means to go through the gates, just these few things as a final summing up of all that we have said about Zion. First of all, going through the gates means to have a true, personal knowledge of the King. Now, I take it for granted that you know that I mean much more than being saved; I mean that we really, each one of us, know the Lord for ourselves. We have got to know Him. There can be no going through the gates if all we are talking about is human relationships, horizontal relationships, and getting to know one another, unless the first and foremost thing is that every one of us has our own clear, intimate, original, personal knowledge and experience of the Lord. He is all the glory of Zion. There is no other glory in Zion. He is all the glory of Zion. His is the grace and the truth that radiates from Zion. It is His glory which is the light, which will lighten all the nations that will walk in the light, in that light. We need to get to know Him. We need to have our own experience of His life and our own experience of His power.

Now hear me on this matter. We need to have our own experience of His life and our own experience of His power. Do not hide in all the other inhabitants of Zion, in all the other daughters of Zion. That includes the brothers as well. The Scripture calls us all "the daughters of Zion." People say this Book [the Bible] is all one-sided, but really it isn't, is it? It always refers to all the men, and they are great men of war some of them, as the daughter of Zion. So ladies, look up; it is not all one-sided. But it is an interesting thing, isn't it, that we have got to really get to know the Lord before we get to know one another?

Is it not interesting how in Colossians 2:19 it says. "... holding fast the Head, from whom the whole body ..." So often we try to get the body and we lose the Head. We need a holding fast of the Head. What does it mean to hold fast the Head? It means you have your own intimate, personal knowledge of the Lord. You have your own experience of the Lord. You have your own understanding of the Lord. You have your own appreciation of the Lord. Now, we need to know His life. We need to know His power. It is no good hiding in one another. You can come into a meeting like this and there is plenty of life. Then you sort of feel, "Oh, I came in a bit dull," so you feel a bit better for it because you have coasted along with the life of everybody else. Do you see? When those days of persecution and trouble come, you are going to be found out. In that day, you will shrivel up and die because you don't have your own experience of the life of the Lord.

Now do not say, "Oh, what do I do? Do I run off into a monastery or convent and sort of shut myself up in a cell for a couple of years and get my own experience?" No, not at all. Just do what you are doing now, only do it with a clear understanding of your problem. Know that you have got to know the Lord yourself and it is no good hiding in the company. How do you stop hiding in the company? Is it by stopping coming to the meeting? No, not at all. That is the way the enemy will get to you. The Scripture says, "Forsake not the assembling of yourselves together and so much the more as you see the day approaching." (Hebrews 10:25). So that is not the way. As we see the Lord coming, do not let the enemy get you on that one or you will be out. What you need to do is to recognise the problem and say, "Well, now, I'm coasting along with these others. I've got to have my own experience. I've got to have my own knowledge of the King."

Real Anointing

It is not only His life, it is also His power. There is an anointing for us, dear friends. Now, people sometimes talk about this anointing, just as if somehow or other, we have all got it, haven't we? Of course, we have all got it since we are all in the body, and the Head is one, our one Head, and the anointing is on the Head. Of course, we all have this anointing. Furthermore, we have this anointing in a church meeting. You see, every time the church gathers, the anointing is there if the leaders and if the responsible folks will sense what that anointing is and follow it. Now, insofar as we follow it, there is life and power in the whole meeting and the will of God is done. But there is a danger that because there is an anointing in the meeting, we tend to think, "Now we've got it," you see. Do you know that in a prayer meeting, the dimmest and most carnal Christian can sometimes pray as if they are absolutely spiritual? I do not know if that has found some of you out, but you see, what happens is this: you can have a meeting and because the meeting is following the anointing, someone who is all fleshly, yet caught up in the meeting's anointing, can absolutely come in with the right words. So we hear, "My, that was a good prayer of So-and-So, not the normal flesh; something of the Lord." But it is not really in them; they are still flesh.

Now, what I am saying is this, and I am speaking generally. There is an anointing for a meeting, but we need a specific anointing. Unless we know the King, who is the Anointed One, you and I will never have a specific and particular anointing. People say to me, "But surely you don't know it, do you? I mean, you take it by faith ..." Oh, that is nonsense, absolute nonsense. I defy anybody who is really anointed to tell me they do not know it. It is the difference between chalk and cheese, between day and night. When a person has received the anointing, they may be still very weak in lots of ways, but something has happened and they know it. Whether it was Watchman Nee, or whether it was D.L. Moody, or Reuben Torrey, or Billy Graham, or anyone else, they will all tell you, "There came a point when something happened to me, when God did something in my life, and I know it."

It is not that you become proud, because you are just as weak and stupid as ever, but something has happened. The Lord has committed Himself in a new way. You see some people are afraid to ask the Lord. They tend to think: "Well, I am the Lord's; I am. Isn't that faith?" Well, it may be ... and it may not be. Sometimes faith is to say, "Dear Lord, I know it's all mine *in You*, but I at present am not experiencing it. There's a lack in my life. I want to be specific. *'Ye have not because ye ask not.'* I want to be specific. I want a specific anointing."

When we begin to ask for a specific anointing, God answers us specifically. We need to have our own experience. We are going to go through the gates. Believe me, this is a battle. We cannot all just drift. We are going to need real, personal knowledge of the Lord. It is no good at all depending on someone if that one is wrong. If they say something, the whole work goes off the rails because there are no other people who have an anointing, who can say, "Just wait, just wait. We're going wrong!" Church history is full of this. Movements that began with the Lord, which are now miles away from the Lord because of some big person in it who has said, "This and this and this," and everyone says, "Yes, yes, yes."

We need real anointing so that we know the mind of the Lord and that kind of anointed fellowship where we can be prodded and restrained, or sometimes pushed, to really do the will of the Lord. A true, personal knowledge of the King; don't you think that is what is needed? I do. I think the beauty of the Lord our God needs to be upon us. When that happens, then the nations round about will take note. They will not see religious people, they will not see fanatical people, but they will see the beauty of the Lord. That is Zion.

A Life Laid Down for the King

Going through the gates means a life laid down for the King. I say that particularly—a life laid down for the King. Going through the gates means that you are not going to live in your nice little farm outside the city, but you are going through the gates into the city where even a garden was not allowed in the old days; you had to have every garden outside the city. You have got to go in, and in one sense, it is a life laid down.

What does it mean, a life laid down? Jesus said, "If any man follow Me, let him deny himself, take up his cross, and follow Me" (Matthew 16:24, Mark 8:34, Luke 9:23). Why did He say "his cross"? Did he mean a kind of migraine or some sort of stomach trouble? Is that your cross? You have got arthritic hips—is that your cross? You have got some allergy; is that your cross? No. Why then did the Lord say, "...take up his cross"? He meant My cross made his; My Calvary made yours. Are you ready?

What does it mean: "Let him deny himself"? It means let him give up all rights to himself as it says in the New English Bible. Let him give up all rights to himself. Now, that is the problem. Haven't we all got rights? Isn't our problem the question of our rights? We like to have our rights and stand on our rights and fight for our rights. A life laid down is simply rights given up for the King.

What does it mean? It means our life is at His disposal. Is your life at His disposal? Really? If the Lord were to say to you in your heart this very moment, "I want you in Patagonia." Are you ready? If the Lord were to say to you, "You did this and this and this, which was wrong, and you harmed So-and-So. I want you to go and say, 'Sorry.'" Are you at His disposal?

You see, we all talk about, "Lord, Lord." We sing, "He is Lord," but when it comes to it, He cannot say, "Go and say sorry ... go and do this ... go and make restitution ... humble yourself on this matter, or go to this place, or that place, or come here." No. When it comes to it, He is Lord in name but not in practice. To go through the gates" means that He is Lord. As His mother once said to those servants, "Whatsoever He says, do it" (John 2:5).

Now, I am not saying that the moment the Lord tells you something, you shouldn't share it in fellowship. If the Lord were to say to you, "Go to Timbuktu," I hope with all my heart that you would share it with your brothers and sisters. I mean, we do not just want people getting on trains first thing tomorrow morning and going to Timbuktu! Then, when they are there saying, "Well, I believe the Lord told me to come to Timbuktu." Let us fellowship in this matter; test this thing out with your brothers and sisters. What I want to know is whether you are really at the disposal of the Lord. That is my point. Can He really do with you what He wants to do?

You see this whole matter of worldliness, as some people call it, is all a matter of His lordship. There are times when the Lord allows a person to do something. Just because So-and-So is permitted to do something, does not mean that you are. It is a question of whether He is Lord in *your* life. You do not know how God dealt with So-and-So in earlier years. You see, much of this matter of giving up things, of letting go of things is because God is really disciplining you. I think that Rees Howells at times may have gone to some extremes but, my word, what the Lord did with him as an object lesson in this matter. He said to him, "Let your hair grow long, or keep your hat on, or do not have it on at all." I mean, weird things, but God was doing something with His servant to see whether He could produce an instrument of intercession that was absolutely at the disposal of the Lord.

Now, there are times when the Lord says to you, "No more football." It does not mean football is wrong. It just means He said to you, "No more football." To others He might say, "No more of the box [TV]." So the Telly has got to go. Now, I don't belong to those who believe the Telly is absolutely the Devil personified, and that he sort of grins out of the screen at every possible opportunity. I thank God for the news commentary, and other documentaries, and many other things that are most instructive and helpful. Yet like a book, like a newspaper, like radio, there are things that are evil and things that are good, and in all of these things we can read newspapers and not read the Word. We can read novels yet never study the Book of books, the Word of God. When that happens, the Lord has to be Lord of a life and say, "This is destroying you. Finish! Out with it."

That is what shows whether we are at His disposal or not. We can sort of say, "Now, this cannot be the Lord; it must be the enemy. I mean, I am getting extreme. So-and-So has a television and a colour one too! So-and-So buys tickets and gives them to others for football matches." That is not the point. The point is what the Lord is saying to *you*. What He let So-and-So do is another matter. What He is doing in your life is something between Him and you. Are you at His disposal? Well, I just underline that, once again.

Fitly Framed Together

I want to go on to something else. What does it mean to go through the gates? It means to be fitly framed together. That is a most unusual phrase to speak of human beings, isn't it? *Fitly framed together*. When I see the size of some, and the smallness of others, I wonder just what it means fitly framed together. I suppose it is rather like a jigsaw puzzle. When a jigsaw puzzle is all in place, it is fitly framed together. The whole thing has found its relationship to all the other pieces, and you see the whole picture.

A house is a whole matter of being fitly framed together. I remember that building inspector coming to Halford House years ago. He was such an ogre and a tiger, but he became such a friend in the end and such a help. When he first came in here, he stumped around saying, "You will have to do this, you will have to do that, you will have to do the other." Then finally, in a great moment of triumph, he stood over here and said, "and the whole of this wall will have to come down."

I said, "The whole of this wall will have to come down?"

"Yes," he said, "the whole of this wall and part of that corner, right about there. It will have to be rebuilt—first of all, a very strong foundation, and then 13 inches thick."

I said, "Thirteen? But," I said, "we don't need a castle."

He said to me, "You don't know if Billy Graham will ever come and speak here."

I said to him, "I don't think Billy Graham will come here."

He said, "Well, you don't know. If Billy Graham came here, they would pack this place so that there wouldn't be room to stand. We're going to build it so they can stand from wall to wall."

Well, now I am very thankful for that building inspector, really, because at that time, we were quite a small company and it just seemed so stupid. Yet, when I have seen the way we have packed this room at times and seen some of the riotous parties that are sometimes held here, I am very glad for that 13 inch wall. It is fitly framed together. Wouldn't it be a terrible thing if it was not fitly framed together? I think some of you might well feel a bit nervous. You could look at all the people and work out their weight. Now I do not want to get personal, but think of it. I mean, let us say there is an average of about seven, eight, nine stone apiece? Should we bring it down? (Some of the ladies may be wincing under my ministry just now), but the point is this: when you work it out, all these people are a large amount of weight. It is a good thing this place is fitly framed together; it can take it all. Praise the Lord!

Now, God is building a house that can take anything. It can bear all the glory, all the glory. When the glory comes in, it won't just disintegrate, because it has been fitly framed together. It is going to be able to take all the glory and radiate all the glory. This Zion that God is building is His eternal administration, His eternal headquarters, His eternal home, His eternal bride. It is not something just for an age. It is not something for just a little bit of time. It is something forever and ever and therefore He is really doing a thorough work.

A Shared Life

Now we can talk about being fitly framed together, but what does it really mean? Well, frankly, it means a life shared. It means that once we have got our own knowledge of the Lord, and we have laid down our life for the King, we have got to have a shared life. If we do not have a shared life, we do not know anything about being fitly framed together.

What does it mean a shared life? It means you just cannot do anything off your own bat. You have got to think of others. Just like a family cannot do everything off their own bat; they have to share. They have to take others into consideration.

Do you understand? This means very simply that we have to open up to one another. That is what we do not always like, do we? I do not mean washing "dirty linen" in public, but what I do mean is that there are times when we have to open up to one another. When we have got needs and problems, we have got to open up.

I remember some of the wonderful prayer times we had recently, how in different prayer groups people opened up and said, "I've got this need. Will you all pray for me?" I think more was done in some of those times than for a long time, just simply because we were able to pray for one another.

When people do not tell us what the need is, or will not open up, how can we be fitly framed together? I look at somebody and think, "Oh, there's So-and-So over there, so prim and proper. They are so correct, never a problem. I wish I was like them. No problems. They're a bit lethargic, but no problems." Then they open up and we find out they have, in fact, got real problems.

For instance, I have heard some lovely testimonies. Now, if I just met some of these dear ones in a meeting, I would not know that there were years and years and years of suffering behind those lives. I would not know the great and deep problems that God touched and marvellously, as it were, solved and brought them through into a new life. But when I know it, doesn't it give me a new appreciation of them? I feel I know them. I feel that now I understand. If there are problems or particular things, I begin to understand a little more of their temperament because they have opened up. We cannot be fitly framed together unless we have opened up to one another. That is what it means. We have got to find relationship to one another. We have got to find our gift, our function.

You see, we cannot be fitly framed together unless the Holy Spirit can manifest Himself, as He will, through one another in the building up of the body of the Lord Jesus.

We all have got something to give. Of course, we need to have that love and care for one another, and oh dear, how often this is lacking. It is as if the enemy comes in and sort of anesthetizes a whole company of believers. It is as if he sort of puts a spiritual cocaine into the bloodstream. Somehow or other we all want to love each other, we want to care for each other, but we feel distant, we feel inhibited, we feel we just cannot do it. That is the kind of bondage that needs to be dragged out into the open and broken in the name of the Lord! Otherwise, the enemy is going to say, "I will not allow this company [of believers] to love each other. I will not allow them to care for one another, I'll just inhibit them all." He does not have to do it through foul insinuation and division and faction. All he has to do is inhibit us so that somehow or another we just feel we cannot do anything, we cannot open up. It needs breaking! We need that love of God shed abroad in our hearts, which cares for one another, is sensitive to one another, that somehow or other watches over one another, not in a busybody manner, but in a really loving manner.

Such being fitly framed together is not going to come about if you are flitting off here and flitting off there. I suppose some people think: "Oh what's *he* talking about? He flits off here and flits off there." But I just remind you, I did have 25 years of it! The thing is that we will not get anywhere by just flitting around, not taking responsibility; not being responsible. When God does this work, it is wonderful.

Well, those are a few thoughts I have had about going through the gates. It really means *every part is functioning*. Every one of us has a part to play. People say to me, "Well, I don't know. I feel terribly young and unable." Learn by experience. Until you learn to open up and learn to contribute and learn to function you are never going to get anywhere. You have to start. When we start, God takes over our education.

Going through the gates. Have you gone through the gates? I know many, many ones who really have committed themselves to the Lord, but I wonder whether what we have said here comes home with a new challenge? You see, we can talk about going through the gates, but what we are committed to is a truth. God preserve us. We need to see truth, but we are not committed to a truth; we are committed to the King. We are committed to that truth being made flesh and blood. May God do this in us all. May He preserve us from just littleness, because that is what could happen. We could all get into our little groups and love each other and care for each other and minister to one another and then in the end, somehow or other lose the whole great objective of God, which is that we should know the rod of His strength going out of Zion, His ruling in the midst of His enemies, and so also the uttermost parts of the earth becoming His possession. May the Lord help us to occupy till He comes and may we really go through those gates and commit ourselves to the Lord, that He may be able to do this work in us.

Shall we pray?

Now, Lord, we just pray together, oh Father, write this upon our hearts. Thou knowest us all Lord. We are all given to apathy or lethargy at one time or another. Lord, wilt Thou bring this word about going through the gates into our hearts in such a vivid and dynamic way that we will not be able to escape it? That we shall know it is the word of the Lord to us? Oh Father, we know that Thou, more than anybody else, want to see this whole matter of Zion worked out in practical circumstances, in practical relationships in our life together. Lord, preserve us we pray, from somehow or other just being caught on different things that are secondary. Help us to see Thy end, and above all Lord, to be committed to Thyself and then to one another. We ask it in the name of our Lord, Jesus. Amen.

Reigning with Christ

Spiritual Character

Talks with Leaders

The Battle of the Ages

The Eternal Purpose of God

The Glory of Thy People Israel

The Gospel of the Kingdom

The Importance of Covering

The Last Days and God's Priorities

The Prize

The Relevance of Biblical Prophecy

The Silent Years

The Supremacy of Jesus

The Uniqueness of Israel

The Way to the Eternal Purpose of God

They Shall Mount up with Wings

Thine Is the Power

Thou Art Mine

Through the Bible with Lance Lambert: Genesis - Deuteronomy

Till the Day Dawns

*Unity : Behold How Good and How Pleasant
- Ministries from Psalm 133*

Warring the Good Warfare

What Is God Doing?: Lessons from Church History

Other books by Lance Lambert

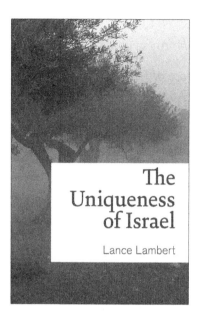

The Uniqueness of Israel

Woven into the fabric of Jewish existence there is an undeniable uniqueness. There is bitter controversy over the subject of Israel, but time itself will establish the truth about this nation's place in God's plan. For Lance Lambert, the Lord Jesus is the key that unlocks Jewish history He is the key not only to their fall, but also to their restoration. For in spite of the fact that they rejected Him, He has not rejected them.

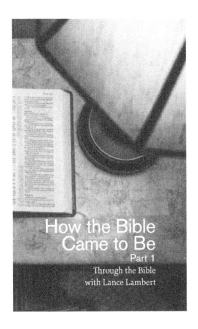

How the Bible Came to Be: Part 1

How is the Bible still as applicable in the 21st century as it was when it was first penned? How did so many authors, with different backgrounds and over thousands of years, write something so perfectly fitting with one another?

Lance Lambert breaks down these, and many other questions in this first volume of his series teaching through the Bible. He lays a firm foundation for going on to study the Word of the living God.

And ye shall seek me, and find me, when ye shall search for me with all your heart.
Jeremiah 29:13

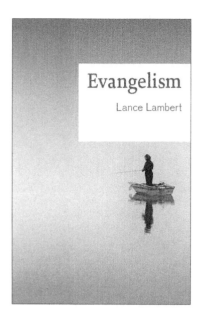

Evangelism

What is God's purpose in evangelism?

It is clear that the Word of God commands us to preach the gospel to every creature, to go into the whole world and make disciples of all nations baptising them in the name of the Father, the Son and the Holy Spirit.

So how do we do it?

In "Evangelism" Lance opens the scriptures to reveal how the church can practically and effectively preach the gospel to the unsaved world, by revealing to them in scripture their need for a Saviour, the work of the Saviour, and how to receive the Saviour. He explains practical means of winning souls and how to follow-up with the newly saved to make disciples of the Lord Jesus. Evangelism is the way by which we gather the materials for the house of God.

So faith comes by hearing, and hearing through the word of Christ.

Ezra-Nehemiah-Esther

"The Bible is not a history book. History is only found in the Scripture when it has something to teach us." (page 62)

Recovery. This key theme throughout the entire timeline of Ezra to Esther gives us a clear vision of the Lord's goal with His people. From the building of Jerusalem and its surrounding walls in Ezra and Nehemiah to the fixing of the irreversible decree of the annihilation of Jews in Esther, the Lord is constantly using His people for recovery. In this book of the series, "Through the Bible with Lance Lambert," we find an in-depth analysis of Ezra, Nehemiah, and Esther, tracing the workings of the Lord throughout history.

Made in the USA
Middletown, DE
14 September 2022